LEAD
TOEFL iBT
SPEAKING

LEAD
TOEFL iBT
SPEAKING

초판1쇄   2021년 04월 01일
개정판1쇄 2022년 04월 07일
개정판2쇄 2024년 12월 07일

지 은 이   DAVID CHIN
번   역   김슬기 박현욱 김은영
디 자 인   최주호(PETER CHOI)
펴 낸 이   박영은
펴 낸 곳   리드에듀북스
등록번호   395-91-01356
전   화   070-4512-5236
팩   스   0504-489-4844
이 메 일   leadedubooks@naver.com
홈페이지   https://leadedubooks.modoo.at
저작권자   DAVID CHIN, 리드에듀북스

Photo Credit ©Shutterstock.com

ISBN   979-11-973714-1-7 13740

값 21,900 원

PREFACE

　토플을 공부하는 학생들의 대부분은 교재의 선택권이 한정되어 있습니다. 점수 향상을 위해서는 다양한 지문을 읽고 수많은 문제를 풀어보아야 하지만, 선택권이 많지 않은 학생들은 불가피하게 비슷한 지문과 문제를 반복해서 풀 수밖에 없는 상황에 놓여 있습니다. 리드 토플은 이러한 상황이 개선되기를 바라는 학생들의 요구를 반영하여 만들어진 책입니다.

　저자인 저는 미국에서 초등, 중등, 고등 교육부터 대학 교육까지 받은 네이티브로서 영어-한국어 이중 언어 구사자입니다. 한국으로 귀국한 뒤 영어교육의 메카인 목동과 대치동에서 토플만을 전문적으로 강의하면서 다양한 강의 자료와 교수법을 직접 연구하고 개발하였으며 수업에 실제로 적용하였습니다. 그러한 과정에서 시중에는 존재하지 않는 새로운 교재 출간의 필요성을 느끼고 리드토플을 집필하였습니다.

　이 책은 기초를 다질 수 있는 연습 문제를 비롯하여, 높은 난이도의 실전 문제까지 세심한 주의를 기울여 설계된 문제들이 실려있습니다. 끊임없는 교재 개발과 연구를 바탕으로 한, 제가 가진 토플에 관한 모든 지식과 노하우가 담긴 책입니다.

　토플을 처음 접하는 학생, 혹은 영어 실력이 중급 수준인 학생들은 실전 문제집을 공부하는 것을 부담스럽게 느끼고 어려워합니다. 문제를 해결하는 스킬을 세심하게 알려주는 본 교재의 컨텐츠 디자인을 따라가면서 다양한 연습문제와 실전문제를 차근차근 풀어 나아간다면 자연스럽게 점수가 향상되는 경험을 하게 될 것입니다.

　앞으로도 풍성한 구성과 질 좋은 컨텐츠를 담아 지속적으로 출간될 리드 토플 교재가 여러분들의 토플 실력 향상에 커다란 밑거름이 되기를 소망합니다.

DAVID CHIN

LEAD
TOEFL iBT
SPEAKING

How to Use This Book

This book has been made to help new test takers understand the different question types first, then apply the speaking templates to respond to the practice questions. After understanding and practicing the four different question types, test takers will then respond to actual tests to further improve their skills and scores.

The speaking section of the TOEFL test requires logical and uninterrupted speech. There should be minimal pauses or buffering while giving the response. Sample responses are given for each practice set, so test takers should first give their response, then compare it with the sample response.

The speaking responses all have time limits, so test takers should practice giving their response to make sure it falls within the time limit.

Preference questions have a time limit of 45 seconds, so test takers should try their best to use all 45 seconds. They should not be satisfied with a 40 second response.

The other three questions are all summary based, which means you might have time left from the 60 seconds, or 60 seconds will not be enough to summarize everything from the reading and listening. Test takers should push themselves to talk faster in these questions.

Like any standardized test, it is best to achieve a top score by studying for the test within a minimal amount of time. Otherwise, the test taker will tire themselves out and eventually give up on their prospective score.

The following chart is a tentative study plan for those who wish to achieve a high score on the TOEFL reading section.

LEAD TOEFL series all follow a 3 week study plan, so it is recommended that test takers use LEAD TOEFL Reading, Listening, and Writing simultaneously while studying for the Speaking section.

The schedule has been balanced with the intention that test takers study for all four sections on a daily basis.

3 Week Study Plan

	Day 1	Day 2	Day 3	Day 4	Day 5
Week 1	Chapter 1 + Practice 1-5	Chapter 1 + Practice 6-10	Chapter 2 + Practice 1-2	Chapter 2 + Practice 3-5	Chapter 3 + Practice 1-2
	Day 6	**Day 7**	**Day 8**	**Day 9**	**Day 10**
Week 2	Chapter 3 + Practice 3-5	Chapter 4 + Practice 1-2	Chapter 4 + Practice 3-5	Chapter 1 + Practice 1-5 (Different opinion)	Chapter 1 + Practice 6-10 (Different opinion)
	Day 11	**Day 12**	**Day 13**	**Day 14**	**Day 15**
Week 3	Actual Test 1	Actual Test 2	Actual Test 3	Actual Test 4	Actual Test 5
Official TOEFL Test					

In the preference question practice, give your prepared response in 45 seconds. If you finish before the 45 second time limit, add details in your response and try again. If you go over the 45 second time limit, eliminate details in your response and try again. After a few attempts, test takers will have a better feel of the time limit and will be able to control their response to finish in the 45 seconds.

For chapters 2 through 4, the responses will be a summary of the reading and listening, or just the listening. If you managed to write down all the details, then the 60 second time limit may not be enough to give your response. So talk fast from the beginning. If you managed to summarize everything and there is time left, there is no need to drag out your response. Just remain quiet until the timer is done.

About the TOEFL iBT

TOEFL (Test of English as a Foreign Language) iBT (Internet-Based Test) is an internet exam for students who speak English as a second language. The test is designed to assess a student's reading, listening, speaking, and writing abilities and how well they understand each section. Thus, the TOEFL test is divided into four sections: Reading, Listening, Speaking, and Writing.

Subject	Content	Time	Score
Reading	2 reading passages. 10 questions per passage	35 minutes	0~30
Listening	2 conversations with 5 questions per conversation 3 lectures with 6 questions per lecture	36 minutes	0~30
Speaking	1 independent 3 integrated	16 minutes	0~30
Writing	1 integrated 1 academic discussion	29 minutes	0~30
		Under 2 hours	0~120

About the TOEFL Speaking Section

Format:

The speaking section of the TOEFL test is divided into four questions. Each question is provided with a preparation time and a response time. Each response is evaluated based on three criteria: delivery (clarity of your speech), language (effective use of grammar and vocabulary), and topic development (the completeness of your response and the coherency of your ideas).

Times:

The first question will have 15 seconds to prepare for your response and 45 seconds to give your response. Questions 2 and 3 will have 30 seconds to prepare and 60 seconds to give your response. Question 4 will have 20 seconds to prepare and 60 seconds to give your response.

Questions:

Question 1 is called independent task and will ask you to give a response based on a familiar topic. Questions 2-4 are called integrated tasks and will require the test taker to read and listen to a topic and integrate their speaking skills.

Table of Contents

CHAPTER
01

Q1 Preference

Q1 Preference

Independent Task

This task requires you to answer a question based on your preference, experience, and knowledge. There is no right or wrong answer; however, you are to present your idea in a logical fashion with supporting details. You will have 15 seconds to prepare for your response and 45 seconds to record your answer.

How the question looks like:

Some people prefer to stay in touch by sending hand written letters. Others prefer to communicate by using the telephone. Which method do you prefer and why?

State whether you agree or disagree with the following statement. Explain your response with specific details and examples.
Learning through your own experience is better than learning from the advice of others.

Do you think computer games influence children in a negative way or a positive way? Include examples and details in your response.

Which of the following trips do you prefer to take?
A trip near your hometown for a long period of time.
A trip far from your hometown for a short period of time.

Why do you get a low score on this question?

There are many reasons why test takers will score low on this question.

1) Not using all 45 seconds:

This question is giving you 45 seconds to respond. You should organize your response so that you are able to speak for all 45 seconds.

2) Response that is cut off:

It is also important to note that giving an incomplete response, which is when your response is cut off at 45 seconds, will give a lower score as well. It is better to give a 40 second response with 5 seconds of silence, than a response where you are cut off.

3) Misreading the question:

Sometimes a single word like "NOT" can lead to a completely different response. The TOEFL test makes simple changes to their questions by changing a few words.

4) Illogical response:

Your response must have coherency and logic. You cannot just mumble or go off on a misdirected response. Make sure your reasons, explanations, and examples are connected and well organized.

5) Unsupported reasons:

Even if you come up with two good reasons for your preference, if you have no example or explanation to back them up, you will get a low score.

6) Misuse of grammar:

Surprisingly, grammar is not the biggest aspect that will undermine your score. Remember, most of the students who take the TOEFL test are non-native English speakers, so their grammar will not be perfect. Still, too many grammar mistakes will result in a low score.

7) Speaking too soft or slow:

Your speaking response is graded either by a human or a computer. If your voice is so soft or slow that the computer cannot understand it, you will get a low score even if the content is perfect.

How to answer step-by-step:

1) Read the question carefully.
2) Identify what the question is asking for.
3) Organize your ideas during the 15 seconds preparation time.
4) Give your response in 45 seconds.

Preparation time:

You will be given 15 seconds to prepare for your response. In reality, you have close to 30 seconds to prepare for your response. This is because everything in the TOEFL test is automated, which also means that the computer will read the question for you. However, reading the question with your eyes is much faster than a computer reading it to you, so while the computer is still reading the question out loud, you can go ahead and start preparing for your response. After the computer has finished reading the question, it will notify the test taker that they will be given 15 seconds to prepare for their response; however, a smart test taker is already preparing for their response at this time.

There is not much you can prepare during the preparation time. Your outline should look something like this:

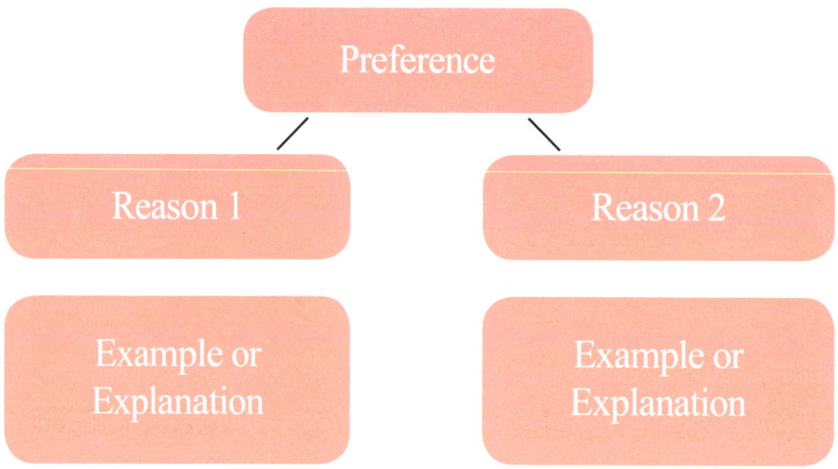

Although most test takers will give a subjective response, it is important to remember that an objective response will be easier to give.

The chart below lists some of the most commonly used reasons in this question type.

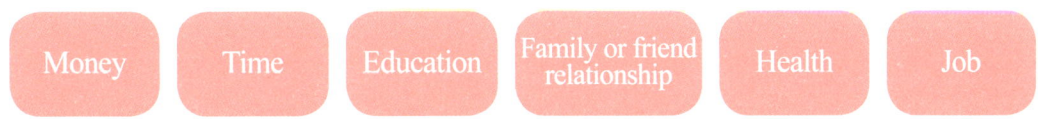

Speaking template:

The TOEFL speaking response should not be spoken casually. Your response should be organized so that it is clear and easy to understand.

Below is a sample of what your response should look like:

Restate the question + Preference	for the following reasons.
To begin with,	Reason 1 .
For example,	Example or explanation .
Furthermore,	Reason 2 .
For instance,	Example or explanation .
Therefore,	Restate the question + Preference .

You do not have to follow the above format word to word. There are other expressions you can use to deliver your response.

Stating your opinion:	I believe that / In my opinion / I prefer
Choosing a side:	I prefer A to B / I would rather choose A than B
Stating the order:	To begin with / Furthermore / Moreover
Stating an example:	For example / For instance / To illustrate
Providing an explanation:	In fact / To be specific / What I mean is
Concluding a response:	Therefore / Thus / As a result

Sample question and response

Do you think computer games influence children in a negative way or a positive way? Include examples and details in your response.

Preparation time: 15 seconds

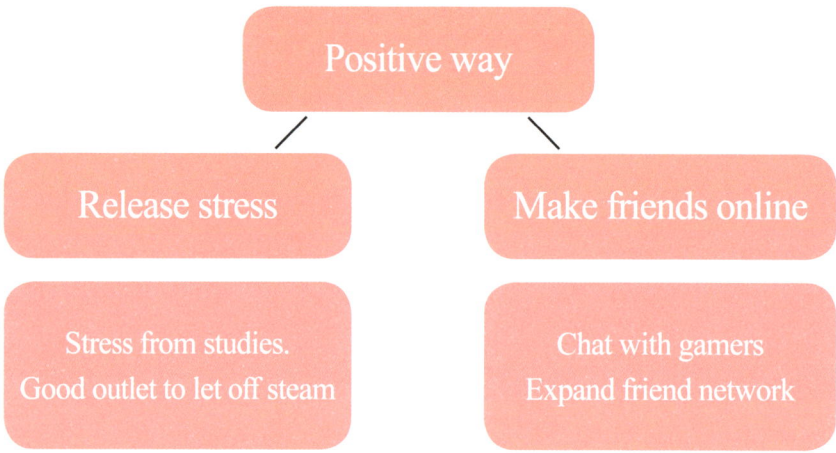

Response time: 45 seconds

I believe that computer games influence children in a positive way for the following reasons.

To begin with, computer games will help children release stress. *To be specific,* children start studying at an early age. They develop stress from their studies, as they study hard to achieve high scores and maintain good grades. This stress can be released by playing computer games, as the purpose for these games is to entertain and let off steam from the player's daily lives.

Furthermore, children will be able to make more friends by playing computer games. *For example,* many players from all over the world meet online to play computer games. They will chat with one another during the game and friendship can be formed during the process. This will expand children's network of friends.

Therefore, these are the reasons why computer games affect children in a positive way.

Practice 1

Do you agree or disagree with the following statement?

Students should be allowed to bring cellphones into the classrooms.

Include examples and details in your response.

PREPARATION TIME
00:00:15

RESPONSE TIME
00:00:45

(CH1-1.mp3)

Notes

Sample response:

I believe that students should be allowed to bring cellphones into the classrooms *for the following reasons.*

To begin with, students should have their phones nearby in cases of family emergency. *For example,* your grandmother could be on her deathbed and if you happened to have the phone with you, you would be able to have your final conversation with your dear grandmother. This would be impossible if your cell phone was not with you in the classroom.

Furthermore, students can stay healthy with the alerts the government sends through the cellphone. *For instance,* due to the Corvid19 pandemic, the government constantly reminds its citizens to wash their hands and keep social distancing. Having a cellphone with you in class will constantly remind you to wash your hands and stay healthy.

Therefore, these are the reasons why students should be allowed to bring cellphones into the classroom.

Practice 2

Is it important to learn about other cultures or ignore them completely?
Include examples and details in your response.

___

PREPARATION TIME
00:00:15

RESPONSE TIME
00:00:45

(CH1-2.mp3)

Notes

Sample response:

I believe that it is important to learn about other cultures *for the following reasons.*

To begin with, your network of friends will grow. *For example,* we live in a global society. It is common to see foreigners walking around in your neighborhood. If you were to learn about their culture, it would be easy to become friends with them and your network of friends will grow. After all, the more friends you have, the better it is.

Furthermore, you will get less stress when you travel. *For instance,* by becoming familiar with other cultures, such as their language and manners, it will prevent you from getting stress when you are traveling. I went to Spain last year and I did not know the language nor manners, so I was under constant stress during my travels because I did not know what I was doing.

Therefore, these are the reasons why it is important to learn about other cultures.

Practice 3

Which quality do you think is important for a member of a team?

1) **Leadership**
2) **Cooperation**
3) **Patience**

Include specific examples and details in your response.

_____

PREPARATION TIME
00:00:15

RESPONSE TIME
00:00:45

(CH1-3.mp3)

Notes

Sample response:

A quality I think that is important for a member of a team is leadership *for the following reasons.*

To begin with, if someone has leadership, it will decrease the level of stress in the team. *For example,* a leader will guide the team in the appropriate direction, giving instructions so that the team members will not have to worry about the project at hand. Thus, the level of stress the team members experience will decrease.

Furthermore, with someone that has leadership, precious time can be saved. *For instance,* most of the time, team members argue and extend the time to complete a task. However, if a leader can appoint tasks to each individual, there will be no argument and the team will be able to carry on the project without wasting time.

Therefore, I believe a quality that makes someone a valuable member of a team is leadership.

Practice 4

Some people prefer to catch up on current events by watching television news. Others prefer to get their news by reading the newspaper. Which method do you prefer?

Include specific examples and details in your response.

PREPARATION TIME
00:00:15

RESPONSE TIME
00:00:45

(CH1-4.mp3)

Notes

Sample response:

I prefer to <u>learn about current events by watching television news</u> *for the following reasons.*

To begin with, <u>it will not be a waste of time.</u> *For example,* <u>as a student, most of my time is invested in doing homework or studying. So watching the television news will help me save time by having the news anchor read the news to me while I do my homework. It would be a waste of time if I were to read the newspaper myself.</u>

Furthermore, <u>watching television news will provide me with only the essential information.</u> *For instance,* <u>news anchors will read the highlights and important details of the news. Newspapers tend to write down every single detail which might not be so important. So a concise news summary would be provided by the television news.</u>

Therefore, these are the reasons why <u>I prefer to watch television news to keep up with current events.</u>

Practice 5

Do you agree or disagree with the following statement?

Friends are the most important influence in one's life.

Include specific examples and details in your response.

PREPARATION TIME
00:00:15

RESPONSE TIME
00:00:45

(CH1-5.mp3)

Notes

Sample response:

I agree that <u>friends are the most important influence in my life</u> *for the following reasons.*

To begin with, <u>I spend the most time with my friends. I go to school with them five days a week, I spend additional hours studying with them at academies, and I also hang out with them during the weekends. With countless hours spent together, it is inevitable that I become influenced by my friends.</u>

Furthermore, <u>my friends influence me because we are in similar situations.</u> *For instance,* <u>as students, we share the burden of maintaining grades. As young adults, we share similar hobbies and interests. Because of similar backgrounds, friends will understand one another and influence each other more.</u>

Therefore, these are the reasons why I believe <u>that friends are the most important influence in my life.</u>

Practice 6

Some people believe that universities should accept students based on their overall grade point average. Others believe that schools should accept students   based on their extracurricular activities. Which do you prefer?

Include specific examples and details in your response.

PREPARATION TIME
00:00:15

RESPONSE TIME
00:00:45

(CH1-6.mp3)

Notes

Sample response:

I believe that <u>universities should accept students based on their overall grade point average</u> *for the following reasons.*

To begin with, <u>a higher grade point average will show better results in universities. After all, the purpose of entering a higher education is to be guaranteed a good job after you graduate. This will only be possible with good grades. So a student that has a high grade point average will have a higher chance of achieving this.</u>

Furthermore, <u>universities should accept students based on their overall grade point average because it will promote the image of the school.</u> *For example,* <u>there is a reason why schools like Harvard or Yale are considered as top tiered schools: they excel in education and maintain smart students. For schools to have or continue this prominent image, they should definitely consider the student's grades.</u>

Therefore, I believe that <u>universities should accept students based on their overall grade point average.</u>

Practice 7

Some people spend their free time alone doing activities such as reading, thinking, or writing. Others spend their free time with people, engaging in group activities like sports. Which do you think is better?

Include specific examples and details in your response.

PREPARATION TIME
00:00:15

RESPONSE TIME
00:00:45

(CH1-7.mp3)

Notes

Sample response:

I prefer to spend my free time alone doing activities such as reading, thinking, or writing *for the following reasons.*

To begin with, it is more cost efficient to spend time alone. *For example,* independent activities like reading a book only requires a book, which can be borrowed from the local library for free. However, group activities such as sports require money to purchase or borrow equipment, as well as renting the field to play on. Also, after playing sports, people usually go out to eat together, which can cost more money.

Furthermore, spending time alone involves less stress. *For instance,* when you are doing something alone, there is no need to accommodate to someone else's schedule or preference. However in a group activity, everyone must meet at the same time and they must all agree on the same activity to play. This might lead to an argument where unnecessary stress will be given.

Therefore, it is more efficient to spend time alone than spend time with other people.

Practice 8

Do you agree or disagree with the following statement?

Students benefit from classes with a larger number of students than they do from smaller classes.

Include examples and details in your response.

PREPARATION TIME
00:00:15

RESPONSE TIME
00:00:45

(CH1-8.mp3)

Notes

Sample response:

I agree that students benefit from classes with a large number of students than they do from smaller classes *for the following reasons.*

To begin with, students will have more opportunities to make new friends. *For example,* a school is not only a place to study, but a place to make good friends. By being in a classroom with a large number of students, they will have more chances to make friends from different backgrounds.

Furthermore, being in a classroom with more students will promote more ideas to be shared. *For instance,* as the famous saying goes, two heads are better than one, with more students, more ideas can be shared because students come from different backgrounds and have diverse experience to share.

Therefore, these are the reasons why being in a classroom with a large number of students is beneficial.

Practice 9

Do you agree or disagree with the following statement?

Reading books is the best way to learn.

Include specific examples and details in your response.

PREPARATION TIME

00:00:15

RESPONSE TIME

00:00:45

(CH1-9.mp3)

Notes

Sample response:

I disagree that reading books is the best way to learn *for the following reasons.*

To begin with, books can be very expensive. *For example,* a typical science book at the university is well worth over a hundred dollars. As students, they will not have much income to purchase such expensive books. There are more cost efficient ways to learn, such as online lectures that are given by famous professors at no charge.

Furthermore, learning by reading a book takes up too much concentration, which most students lack. *For instance,* reading a book may take hours to read and understand. However, students typically lack this concentration because they would rather play outside or hang out with their friends. Rather, a hands on experience engages the student in the study, so they will concentrate fully on the lesson.

Therefore, these are the reasons why reading books is not the best way to learn.

Practice 10

Do you prefer to keep and collect items, or throw them away and purchase new items every time?

Include specific examples and details in your response.

PREPARATION TIME
00:00:15

RESPONSE TIME
00:00:45

(CH1-10.mp3)

Notes

Sample response:

I prefer to <u>keep and collect items</u> *for the following reasons.*

To begin with, <u>keeping and collecting items will save money and at times make profit.</u> *For example,* <u>many people throw away old toys, but these toys can be given to charity or a younger sibling, so the accepting party will not have to pay for a toy. Also, some toys increase in value over the years, so the owner can profit two or three times its original value after a few years.</u>

Furthermore, <u>I prefer to keep and collect items for sentimental reasons.</u> *For instance,* <u>many memories I have are stored in objects. When I listen to old vinyl records, I remember the first time I listened to the song with my wife. Or when I look at the old worn out children's shoe, I recollect my son taking his first steps.</u>

Therefore, these are the reasons why <u>I keep and collect items.</u>

Vocabulary:

logical	adj.	characterized by or capable of clear, sound reasoning.	*rational, analytical*
coherency	adj.	the quality of being logical and consistent.	*consistency, logicality*
undermine	v.	lessen the effectiveness, power, or ability of, especially gradually or insidiously.	*weaken, compromise*
native	n.	a person born in a specified place or associated with a place by birth, whether subsequently resident there or not.	*local, aborigine*
automated	adj.	operated by largely automatic equipment.	
subjective	adj.	based on or influenced by personal feelings, tastes, or opinions.	*personal, emotional*
objective	adj.	(of a person or their judgment) not influenced by personal feelings or opinions in considering and representing facts.	*impartial, unbiased*
casual	adj.	made or done without much thought or premeditation.	*impromptu, spontaneous*
outlet	n.	a means of expressing one's talents, energy, or emotions.	*release*
steam	n.	energy and momentum or impetus.	*energy, vigor*
deathbed	n.	the bed where someone is dying or has died.	
pandemic	adj.	(of a disease) prevalent over a whole country or the world.	*widespread, epidemic*
extend	v.	cause to last longer.	*continue, carry on*
appoint	v.	assign a job or role to (someone).	*nominate, designate*

essential	adj.	absolutely necessary; extremely important.	*crucial, necessary*
concise	adj.	giving a lot of information clearly and in a few words; brief but comprehensive.	*succinct, brief*
inevitable	adj.	certain to happen; unavoidable.	*inescapable*
burden	n.	a duty or misfortune that causes hardship, anxiety, or grief; a nuisance.	*liability, obligation*
extracurricular	adj.	(of an activity at a school or college) pursued in addition to the normal course of study.	
promote	v.	further the progress of (something, especially a cause, venture, or aim); support or actively encourage.	*encourage, assist*
top tier	adj.	of the highest level or quality.	
prominent	adj.	important; famous.	*distinguished, leading*
engage	v.	participate or become involved in.	*join, participate*
accommodate	v.	fit in with the wishes or needs of.	*oblige, assist*
diverse	adj.	showing a great deal of variety; very different.	*various, multiple*
typical	adj.	characteristic of a particular person or thing.	*characteristic, usual*
income	n.	income	*salary, wage*
lack	n.	the state of being without or not having enough of something.	*absence, deficiency*
charity	n.	an organization set up to provide help and raise money for those in need.	*welfare, relief*
sentimental	adj.	of or prompted by feelings of tenderness, sadness, or nostalgia.	*nostalgic, emotional*

CHAPTER
02

Q2 Announcement
and Opinion

Q2 Announcement and Opinion

Integrated Task

In this question type, you are to summarize either a student letter or an announcement from a university and a student's opinion regarding the matter. Points will be given based on how well you can summarize the main idea, as well as the details mentioned in the reading and the listening. You will have 30 seconds to prepare for your response and 60 seconds to record your answer.

How the question looks like:

> The woman expresses her opinion regarding the announcement made by the university. State her opinion and the reasons she gives for holding that opinion.

> The woman expresses her opinion regarding the announcement about the new dormitory. State her opinion and explain the reasons she gives for holding that opinion.

> The man expresses his opinion regarding the student's letter. State his opinion and explain the reasons he gives for holding that opinion.

Why do you get a low score on this question?

There are many reasons why test takers will score low on this question.

1) Response that is cut off:
   It is important to note that giving an incomplete response, which is when your response is cut off at 60 seconds, will give a lower score. It is better to give a 55 second response with 5 seconds of silence, than a response where you are cut off.

2) Summarizing the wrong person:
   Very rarely, test takers will summarize the wrong person's opinion. Make sure you are summarizing the correct person.

3) Lack of details:
   This response is based on how well you can summarize the reading and the listening. Be sure to take good notes while reading the passage and listening to the conversation, and mention those details in your response.

4) Information that was not mentioned:
   Sometimes, test takers will include information that was not mentioned in the reading and the listening. They tend to do this because they might have background information or personal experience on the matter, or they might have misheard the information. Only include information covered in the reading and listening.

5) Unorganized response:
   A reading's summary should be given first, followed by the listening. Follow the speaking template for this question type.

6) Misuse of grammar:
   Surprisingly, grammar is not the biggest aspect that will undermine your score. Remember, most of the students who take the TOEFL test are non-native English speakers, so their grammar will not be perfect. Still, too many grammar mistakes will result in a low score.

7) Speaking too soft or slow:
   Your speaking response is graded either by a human or a computer. If your voice is so soft or slow that the computer cannot understand it, you will get a low score even if the content is perfect.

How to answer step-by-step:

1) Read the university announcement or student letter for 45 seconds. Take notes because the reading passage will not appear again.
2) Listen to a conversation between two students. Take organized notes because the conversation will only be played once.
3) Prepare your response in 30 seconds. During this time, you can organize the notes you took, or practice giving your response.
4) Give your response in 60 seconds.

Notetaking:

It is important to take organized notes, so before you start the speaking section, it is recommended to prepare for your notes. Your notes for this question type should be organized in the following manner:

Reading:

Announcement/Student letter main idea:
Detail 1:
Detail 2 :

Listening:

Man	Woman
Opinion:	Opinion:
Reason 1:	Reason 1:
Details:	Details:
Reason 2:	Reason 2:
Details:	Details:

Reading section:

During the 45 seconds allotted, you must first identify if the reading passage is an announcement or a student letter. This is easy to identify:

1) A university announcement will have a title at the top. Also it will not use first person pronouns like I, me, we, or us.
2) A student letter will start with an address to someone or a group and finish with who it is from. Sometimes, first person pronouns like I, me, we, or us will be used.

The next thing test takers must do is find the main idea of the reading passage.

1) A university announcement's main idea can be found succinctly described in the title. An elaborate more detailed main idea can be found either in the first sentence of the passage, or in the second sentence.
2) A student letter's main idea can be found either in the first sentence of the letter or in the second sentence.

Lastly, if you have time remaining from the 45 seconds, try to write one or two minor details to provide a solid summary of the reading. The details are usually reasons or effects of the main idea.

Example:

Reading time: 45 seconds

Campus Tour Guides

For a long time, campus tour guides have been led by the faculty for prospective students wishing to attend the university. However, starting next semester, university students themselves will be leading the tours. The faculty simply do not have the time to lead campus tours anymore. They need to focus their resources on other important matters and do not have the manpower to do campus tours. Furthermore, the university believes that the university students will be able to provide valuable insight, one that faculties will not have.

Notetaking:

Announcement: *campus tours will be led by university students starting next semester.*

Detail 1: *university faculty do not have the resources nor manpower to lead the tours.*

Detail 2: *university student tour guides will offer valuable insight.*

Listening section:

The conversation will be a little over a minute. You will have to listen to a conversation between two students discussing the announcement or letter. Your job is to write down everything the students say. It is important to write the minor details because a perfect score on this question will have even the smallest details that were mentioned in the conversation.

(CH2-Example.mp3)

Now listen to two students discussing the article.

Man: So what are your thoughts on the matter?

Woman: I think it's a great idea, something that should have happened a long time ago.

Man: Why is that?

Woman: I recently went to the faculty office to get information on a class, and everyone in the office was so busy. It wasn't the first time I saw this too. Every time I went to the office to ask administrative questions, the faculty were either busy answering phone calls, helping long lines of students, or working behind piled sheets of forms. It seems like not having to lead the tours will give them a break.

Man: I didn't know they were so busy…

Woman: Also, the part about valuable insight offered by university students

Man: mm hmm?

Woman: I think university students can really offer valuable information. I know I have a lot of experience I can share with upcoming freshmen. I remember when I attended the campus tour before coming to the school. The faculty leading the tour was nice, but he was not able to answer some of the questions students asked.

Man: Like what?

Woman: Practical ones actually. Which cafeteria serves the best food. Which dormitory is the quietest. Which library has the best studying environment. Things like that. Questions that the faculty member would not have first-hand experience.

Man: I see. I guess our point of view might be more helpful.

Notetaking:

Man	Woman
Opinion:	Opinion: *Great idea*
Reason 1:	Reason 1: *Faculty is very busy*

Details:	Details:
	Recently went to the office
	    - Answering phone calls
	    - Helping lines of students
	    - Working behind piles of forms
	Not leading tours give them break

Reason 2:	Reason 2: *Student can offer valuable insight*

Details:	Details:
	Much experience to share
	Campus tour experience: faculty
	guide could not answer some q's
	    - Cafeteria good
	    - Dorm quiet
	    - Library study
	Faculty not have first-hand
	experience

Speaking template:

The delivery of the summary should start with the reading and end with the listening.

According to the announcement, Announcement + Details .

(OR)

According to the student letter, Main idea + Details .

In the conversation, the (man / woman) (agrees / disagrees) with the (announcement / student letter) for the following reasons.

To begin with, Reason 1 + Details .

Furthermore, Reason 2 + Details .

Therefore, these are the reasons why the (man / woman) (agrees / disagrees) with the (university announcement / student letter).

You do not have to follow the above template word to word. There are other expressions you can use to deliver your response.

Stating the announcement:	According to the announcement
	In regards to the university posting
	The university announcement states that
Stating the letter:	According to the student letter
	The student in the letter writes that
	The letter to the school states that
Stating the opinion:	Agrees with / Supports
	Disagrees with / Not Support
Stating the order:	To begin with / Furthermore / Moreover
Concluding a response:	Therefore / Thus / As a result

Question:

The woman expresses her opinion about the university's plan. Briefly summarize the plan. Then state her opinion about the plan and explain the reasons she gives for holding that opinion.

Sample response:

The university announcement states that current students will lead campus tours for prospective students. Before, the faculty did this, but they no longer have time to lead the tours. The current students will offer unique and valuable insight to the visitors.

In the conversation, the woman agrees with the announcement for the following reasons. To begin with, she has been to the faculty office before, and every time she has been there, they have been really busy. The staff members are busy answering phone calls, helping students in long lines, and attending to piles of paperwork. The woman believes that faculty not having to lead the tours will give them a break.

Furthermore, she believes that university students will be able to provide valuable insight. She has much experience to pass on. When she was in the tour long ago, the man leading it was nice, but there were questions he was unable to answer from experience. Practical questions like which cafeteria has good food, which dormitory is the quietest, or which library is the best place to study. The faculty simply did not have first-hand experience to answer such questions.

Therefore, these are the reasons why the woman agrees with the announcement.

Remember that you have 30 seconds to prepare for your response. Use this time wisely. You can either organize your notes by connecting ideas or ordering the summary of information. Or start practicing your response by speaking out loud. Going over the response in your head is different compared to the response that is verbally spoken. 30 seconds will not be enough to complete the entire response, but at least you are able to practice for half the time before you give your complete response.

Practice 1

Reading Time: 45 seconds

International News

For the past few years, the university campus newspaper has included a one-page column consisting of international news that covered a few of the major stories around the world. However, this section will be removed starting next month. One of the reasons for this change is because other news sources are able to do a better job providing more detailed information and more up-to-date news coverage than the campus newspaper. Furthermore, the elimination of the international news section would create space for a new calendar page, which would list events and activities happening on campus.

(CH2-1.mp3)

The woman expresses her opinion about the plan to eliminate the international news section. Explain her opinion and the reasons she gives for holding that opinion.

PREPARATION TIME
00:00:30

RESPONSE TIME
00:00:60

Reading notes:

Announcement:
Detail 1:
Detail 2:

Conversation notes:

Man	Woman
Opinion:	Opinion:
Reason 1:	Reason 1:
Details:	Details:
Reason 2:	Reason 2:
Details:	Details:

Response:

Sample response:

The university announcement states that starting next month, the international news section will be eliminated from the daily campus newspaper. The reason for this change is that other news sources are better able to provide wider and more up-to-date international news coverage. Also, the elimination will create space for a new calendar page that will list events and activities around campus.

In the conversation, the woman agrees with the announcement for the following reasons.

To begin with, she states that hardly anyone reads the international news section. The section only shows minimal news and most students already know of the news before it is printed on the paper. She believes that the outside sources' coverage is better as well. She inputs that the newsletter should just focus on campus news.

Furthermore, the woman states that campus events and news are posted everywhere so it's hard to keep track of it. She sees announcements posted, but forgets half the time. With the new section, she can cut it out from the newspaper, carry it around, and check to see what's taking place when and where.

Therefore, these are the reasons why the woman agrees with the university announcement.

Practice 2

Reading Time: 45 seconds

Shutting down the Campus Coffeehouse

I believe that the campus coffeehouse should be closed by the university. Don't get me wrong, the coffeehouse is a great place to meet up with friends over a cup of coffee. But no one uses the campus coffeehouse. Every time I walk by the coffeehouse, I see empty seats and tables. The coffeehouse is a waste of space that could otherwise be used for something more useful. Furthermore, the food that is served there is not delicious. The last time I went there with my friend, the muffins and cakes that we ordered were dry and lacked flavor.

Sincerely,
Thomas Johnson

(CH2-2.mp3)

The woman expresses her opinion about the student's letter to the editor. Explain her opinion and the reasons she gives for holding that opinion

PREPARATION TIME
00:00:30

RESPONSE TIME
00:00:60

Reading notes:

Announcement:
Detail 1:
Detail 2:

Conversation notes:

Man	Woman
Opinion:	Opinion:
Reason 1:	Reason 1:
Details:	Details:
Reason 2:	Reason 2:
Details:	Details:

Response:

Sample response:

The student letter states that the campus coffeehouse should be closed. This is because students are not using the coffeehouse and there are lots of empty tables whenever he passes by. Also, the food there does not taste so great.

In the conversation, the woman disagrees with the letter for the following reasons.

To begin with, she likes the fact that the coffeehouse is never crowded, so it is a great place to study. She goes there a lot to read a book or work on a paper for class since it is never noisy. She and other students prefer the coffeehouse over the library as a place to study for their final exams since they can also eat while they work.

Furthermore, the woman believes that the writer has not been to the coffeehouse recently. She admits that the food was not great in the past, but it's better now because the coffeehouse has a new manager and has improved the quality of the food. The woman was there last week and said the food was delicious. Also, the new manager has added healthy foods and snacks so it tastes good and is good for you.

Therefore, these are the reasons why the woman disagrees with the student letter.

Practice 3

Reading Time: 45 seconds

Separate Graduation

Since the beginning, the university has been holding a single ceremony for all the graduating students, where they were given their diplomas. However, starting this year, the university will have two separate graduation ceremonies. Half of the graduating class will attend the ceremony on the first day, and the other half will attend the ceremony the next day. There are two reasons for this change. First, with the increase in student enrollment and the diplomas being handed out to each student, the ceremony has become too long. Furthermore, the ceremony hall where they hold the graduation is too small to accommodate the audience members.

(CH2-3.mp3)

The woman expresses her opinion about the university announcement. Explain her opinion and the reasons she gives for holding that opinion

PREPARATION TIME
00:00:30

RESPONSE TIME
00:00:60

Reading notes:

Announcement:
Detail 1:
Detail 2:

Conversation notes:

Man	Woman
Opinion:	Opinion:
Reason 1:	Reason 1:
Details:	Details:
Reason 2:	Reason 2:
Details:	Details:

Response:

Sample response:

The university announcement states that beginning this year, the university will hold two graduation ceremonies. The reason for this change is that the number of students has increased in recent years and so the ceremony would be too long. Also, the ceremony hall will be too small to accommodate the large number of students with their family and friends.

In the conversation, the woman disagrees with the announcement for the following reasons.

To begin with, she believes that it is unnecessary. She agrees that it will take a long time for the students to receive the diplomas individually, but she believes that an easier way to reduce time is to decrease the number of speeches. Students, professors, administrators, and the president of the university all give speeches, which she finds unnecessary.

Furthermore, the woman believes that the size of the hall is not the problem, rather the students invite too many people. The school should reduce the number of guests students can invite. Currently, graduating students can invite 10 people, which is too many compared to 4 or 5 people other schools have their students invite. The woman believes that inviting 6 people will be adequate and the ceremony can stay as it is.

Therefore, these are the reasons why the woman disagrees with the university announcement.

Practice 4

Reading Time: 45 seconds

Meetings With Advisors Not To Be Required

Currently, the university has made it mandatory for students to meet with their academic advisors before the start of each semester. Advisors help students on choosing which courses to take, as well as help them on graduation requirements. Unfortunately, I do not see the point of these meetings, since the information about the courses is already posted in the university website. Also, without having to meet with the advisors, students would not have to go through the trouble of scheduling a meeting when they are both free.

Sincerely, Sarah Johnson

(CH2-4.mp3)

The man expresses his opinion regarding the proposal in the letter. Summarize the proposal, then state the man's opinion and explain the reasons he gives for holding that opinion.

PREPARATION TIME
00:00:30

RESPONSE TIME
00:00:60

Reading notes:

Announcement:

Detail 1:

Detail 2:

Conversation notes:

Man	Woman
Opinion:	Opinion:
Reason 1:	Reason 1:
Details:	Details:
Reason 2:	Reason 2:
Details:	Details:

Response:

Sample response:

The student letter states that she doesn't see the point of advisory meetings. The information about the courses can already be found on the university's website and there is also the difficulty of finding a time to meet with the advisor when they are both free.

In the conversation, the man disagrees with the letter for the following reasons.

To begin with, he states that it's not the same information that are found on the website. The basic information is there, but advisors provide more than that. There are different requirements to meet a graduation, like different classes. By talking to someone, that person can help figure that out. Advisors have lots of extra information, so they make it easier to see what the choices are.

Furthermore, the man never had trouble scheduling a meeting. If anyone has trouble, they are waiting till the last minute to set up a meeting. If students call or go to the office early, meeting times are available. Waiting till the last moment makes it harder to meet with the advisor.

Therefore, these are the reasons why the man disagrees with the student letter.

Practice 5

Reading Time: 45 seconds

Electronic Textbooks

Starting early next year, the university will be switching to electronic textbooks from the traditional-bound textbooks. Students will be able to use their device to download their course textbook and read the material directly from their device. Although the cost of the electronic device is around $200, this will be a one-time payment. Students will be able to save money in textbook, considering its rising costs in recent years. Electronic books for classes will definitely be much cheaper than buying regular textbooks. Also, the school believes that the electronic textbook will be a great study tool since it will be easy to operate and has features such as highlighting text and note-taking.

(CH2-5.mp3)

The woman expresses her opinion about the university's plan. Briefly summarize the plan then state her opinion and explain the reasons she gives for holding that opinion.

PREPARATION TIME
00:00:30

RESPONSE TIME
00:00:60

Reading notes:

Announcement:
Detail 1:
Detail 2:

Conversation notes:

Man	Woman
Opinion:	Opinion:
Reason 1:	Reason 1:
Details:	Details:
Reason 2:	Reason 2:
Details:	Details:

Response:

Sample response:

The university announcement states that the school will be switching from traditional bound textbooks to electronic textbooks early next year. Students will only have to pay a one-time expense for the electronic device. The device is simple to operate and offers many features to make it an effective study aid.

In the conversation, the woman disagrees with the announcement for the following reasons.

To begin with, she states that the cost is not realistic. She admits that textbooks are not cheap, but she thinks that students will not just use one device the whole time. If the device breaks, students will have to purchase another one, or if the device is upgraded with a fancy feature, students would want to upgrade. If students replace the device every year, the cost will add up.

Furthermore, not everyone will benefit from the device. It will only be helpful if the students know how to use it. The device is small, only 18 or 20 centimeters tall. The keypad and control buttons are small too. So those with a normal sized finger will have trouble selecting the item or getting it to function properly. So there is nothing good to come from the fancy features if users are unable to use them. The woman prefers the old fashioned way of taking notes on the page and underlining or highlighting important sections of the book.

Therefore, these are the reasons why the woman disagrees with the announcement.

Vocabulary:

regarding	prep.	with respect to; concerning.	*concerning, in regard to*
rare	adj.	(of an event, situation, or condition) not occurring very often.	*infrequent, scarce*
undermine	v.	lessen the effectiveness, power, or ability of, especially gradually or insidiously.	*sabotage, compromise*
succinct	adj.	(especially of something written or spoken) briefly and clearly expressed.	*compact, condensed*
elaborate	adj.	involving many carefully arranged parts or details; detailed and complicated in design and planning.	*complicated, intricate*
faculty	n.	the teaching staff of a university or college, or of one of its departments or divisions, viewed as a body.	
prospective	adj.	(of a person) expected or expecting to be something particular in the future.	*future, eventual*
manpower	n.	the number of people working or available for work or service.	*workers, labor pool*
insight	n.	the capacity to gain an accurate and deep intuitive understanding of a person or thing.	*intuition, perception*
elimination	n.	the complete removal or destruction of something.	*destruction, eradication*
minimal	adj.	of a minimum amount, quantity, or degree; negligible.	*minimum, least*

reduce	v.	make smaller or less in amount, degree, or size.	*lessen, decrease*
adequate	adj.	satisfactory or acceptable in quality or quantity.	*enough, ample*
mandatory	adj.	required by law or rules; compulsory.	*obligatory, required*
operate	v.	(of a person) control the functioning of (a machine, process, or system).	*work, utilize*
fancy	adj.	elaborate in structure or decoration.	*elaborate*

Additional vocabulary:

Chapter notes:

CHAPTER
03

Q3 General to Specific

Q3 General to Specific

Integrated Task

In this question type, you are to summarize the academic reading passage and a lecture related to the reading. Points will be given based on how well you can summarize the main idea, as well as the details mentioned in the reading and the listening. You will have 30 seconds to prepare for your response and 60 seconds to record your answer.

How the question looks like:

The professor talks about car factories. Explain how it is related to the fourth industrial revolution.
The reading passage talks about the fourth industrial revolution, while the lecture discusses about car factories.

The professor gives his experience of working as a waiter. Explain how it is related to cooperation.
The reading passage talks about cooperation, while the lecture discusses about the professor working as a waiter.

The professor talks about online games. Explain how it is related to social network.
The reading passage talks about social network, while the lecture discusses about online games.

Why do you get a low score on this question?

There are many reasons why test takers will score low on this question.

1) Response that is cut off:

    It is important to note that giving an incomplete response, which is when your response is cut off at 60 seconds, will give a lower score. It is better to give a 55 second response with 5 seconds of silence, than a response where you are cut off.

2) Lack of details:

    This response is based on how well you can summarize the reading and the listening. Be sure to take good notes while reading the passage and listening to the lecture, and mention those details in your response.

3) Information that was not mentioned or phrased incorrectly:

    Sometimes, test takers will include information that was not mentioned in the reading and the listening. They tend to do this because they might have background information or personal experience on the matter, or they might have misheard the information. Only include information covered in the reading and listening. Also, information can be said incorrectly. Try your best to understand what was mentioned.

4) Unorganized response:

    A reading's summary should be given first, followed by the listening. Follow the speaking template for this question type.

5) Misuse of grammar:

    Surprisingly, grammar is not the biggest aspect that will undermine your score. Remember, most of the students who take the TOEFL test are non-native English speakers, so their grammar will not be perfect. Still, too many grammar mistakes will result in a low score.

6) Speaking too soft or slow:

    Your speaking response is graded either by a human or a computer. If your voice is so soft or slow that the computer cannot understand it, you will get a low score even if the content is perfect.

How to answer step-by-step:

1) Read the academic passage for 50 seconds. Take notes because the reading passage will not appear again.
2) Listen to the lecture. Take organized notes because the lecture will only be played once.
3) Prepare your response in 30 seconds. During this time, you can organize the notes you took, or practice giving your response.
4) Give your response in 60 seconds.

Notetaking:

It is important to take organized notes, so before you start the speaking section, it is recommended to prepare for your notes. Your notes for this question type should be organized in the following manner:

Reading:

Title of the reading passage:

Definition or description of the title:

Detail:

Listening:

Lecture's point 1:

Detail:

Lecture's point 2:

Detail:

Reading section:

The reading passage will discuss the general idea of the lecture. Think of it as the background information before the lecture is given.

When the reading passage comes out, write down the title of the passage first. The title is the main idea of the reading passage, as well as the lecture. Then, quickly find the definition or description of the title in the reading passage.

The most common way a definition or description is stated: "(TITLE) is …"

In the remaining 50 seconds, try to write down a supporting detail from the reading.

Example:

Reading time: 50 seconds

Irrational Commitment

When individuals spend a great deal of time working on a project, they want to see a positive result. However, they may become so attached to producing a positive outcome that even if the process starts to show a failing work, the individuals will ignore the facts and work harder to produce a good result. This is known as irrational commitment. This tendency to progress with a project when it is actually better to quit can be particularly strong when people feel they may be assessed by others for their likely success or failure.

Notetaking:

Title of the reading passage: *irrational commitment*

Definition or description of the title: *people become so attached to producing a positive outcome that even if the process starts to show a failing work, they will continue with the project to produce a good result.*

Detail: *particularly strong if people feel they will be judged by their success or failure.*

Listening section:

The lecture will discuss a specific example or topics regarding the reading passage. Most of the time, the lecture will mention two points regarding the general topic. Sometimes however, the professor may give a lengthy personal experience supporting the general topic. Regardless, be thorough in taking notes.

The lecture will be under 2 minutes. It is essential that you try to write down as much information as you can. This includes names and numbers, as well as adjectives that were used to describe the object. Remember, the more you summarize, the more points you will get.

(CH3-Example.mp3)

Listen to part of a lecture from a psychology class.

Professor:
Let me give you a personal example. A few years ago, my wife and I were looking for a house to buy. We found one we liked, out in the country. But my wife was hesitant in purchasing the house. The house was not in the best condition and probably would need some repairs. But I really felt good about the house, especially the architecture and the unusual way it was built. So I finally convinced my wife we could hire people to fix up the place. We would come to live in the house after it was repaired.

Well, the workers who came to repair the house soon discovered other problems we were not aware of. The roof was damaged and would require expensive repairs. When the workers finished fixing the roof, they discovered that the house had electrical problems. Most of the wires had to be replaced, which would be costly. My wife reminded me of her hesitation to buy the house, however, I was more determined to make the house mine. I paid for the repairs to be done. But it actually got worse...

Insects had eaten through some of the walls, so the walls had to be torn out and replaced. Replacing the walls would actually be more expensive than all the other repairs, but at this point, I felt like a mission to finish repairing the house no matter what the cost. If I stop, I felt that my wife would nag at me for not following her advice!

Notetaking:

Prof's personal ex:

Few years ago: look for house to buy w/ wife → out in country

BUT wife hesitant (x good cond. + need repairs)

Prof felt good about house, esp. arch. + unusual way built.

Convince wife → fix house → live in it after

Workers discover other problems.

Damaged roof. $ to repairs

Elec problems. Wires need replace → $

Wife remind hesitance. BUT prof more determined to buy house. Pay for repairs

Worse

Insects eat thru walls. Torn out and replaced. Most $ repair.

At this point: mission to finish repair.

If stop, wife would nag.

This particular lecture gives a lengthy experience the professor had. This means that in your speaking template, you should NOT divide your response into two points by mentioning the phrases "To begin with" and "Furthermore".

Remember, every detail counts. Your notes should include which parts of the house needed repairs, the order the professor mentions, what caused the walls to be repaired, and ultimately, the last part of the lecture why the professor was hesitant of stopping the repairs.

Question:

Explain how the example from the professor's lecture illustrates irrational commitment

Speaking template:

The delivery of the summary should start with the reading and end with the listening.

The reading passage talks about Reading Title, which is Definition or Description.
It also states that   Detail   .
In the lecture, the professor goes in detail regarding   Reading Title   .
To begin with,   Point 1 + Details   .
Furthermore,   Point 2 + Details   .
(These / This) (are / is) the (examples / example) the professor uses to explain Reading Title.

You do not have to follow the above template word to word. There are other expressions you can use to deliver your response.

Stating the reading:	The reading passage talks about
	The academic reading discusses
Stating the lecture:	In the lecture, the professor goes into detail
	The professor goes on to describe
Stating the order:	To begin with / Furthermore / Moreover

Sample response:

The reading passage discusses the concept of <u>irrational commitment, which is when individuals grow attached to the idea of a successful outcome, that even if it looks like the project will fail and the disadvantages outweigh the benefits, they will still continue their project and not give up. This irrational commitment can be especially strong if they feel they may be judged by others for their success or failure.</u>

In the lecture, the professor <u>gives a personal example. A few years ago, he and his wife were looking for a house to buy. They found an old house out in the country, but his wife had her doubts, as the house was not in a good condition and needed repairs. However, the professor fell in love with the architecture of the house. So the professor convinced his wife that they can hire people to fix the house. They decided to buy the house and live after the repairs were finished. However, the workers discovered that things were worse than what the professor originally thought. The roof was damaged and needed expensive repairs. The workers also found electrical problems. Most of the wires had to be replaced, which would be expensive. At that point, the professor's wife reminded him of the doubts she had earlier. But the professor was more determined than ever and paid the wiring to be replaced. However, to make matters worse, they found that insects had eaten through some of the walls and the walls had to be torn out and replaced. This would be more expensive than all the other repairs. Still, the professor thought to himself that he had to see this through, otherwise he thought his wife would nag at him for not following her advice.</u>

This is the example the professor uses to explain <u>irrational commitment.</u>

Most of the time, the lecture will include two points regarding the general idea of the reading passage. In that case, you should divide the points by mentioning the phrases "To begin with" and "Furthermore".

Remember to prepare your response during the 30 seconds. Organize your notes or better yet, practice giving your response out loud.

Practice 1

Reading Time: 50 seconds

Reference Groups

People influence the way we think and behave. We tend to copy the behavior and attitudes of the people we admire and respect. These people whom we respect and whose behavior and attitudes we tend to copy are known as reference groups. Reference groups provide a frame of reference that can influence how we think and behave. Over a long period of time, we may be influenced by various reference groups. As we age, or come across new environments, our reference groups may change, which also leads our attitudes and behavior to a new direction.

(CH3-1.mp3)

Using the example from the lecture, explain how people's behavior is influenced by reference groups.

PREPARATION TIME
00:00:30

RESPONSE TIME
00:00:60

Reading notes:

Title:

Definition or description:

Detail:

Lecture notes:

Lecture's point 1:

Detail:

Lecture's point 2:

Detail:

Response:

Sample response:

The reading passage discusses the concept of <u>reference groups, who are groups of people individuals admire and respect that they try to imitate their behavior and attitudes. As people grow older, their reference groups may change and their attitudes and behavior will change accordingly.</u>

In the lecture, the professor <u>gives his personal experience. When he began his university studies, he became friends with art students. They were older, fun, and creative and so the professor thought they were cool. The art students dressed casually, in t-shirts and jeans, and wore that wherever they went. So the professor started to wear like that too and he felt right in and he himself felt cool. Later the professor graduated, moved to Chicago and got a job there. He worked with some bright people at his new job who had been working at the company for a few years already. They were handling major responsibilities and the professor was really impressed. Sometimes, they would get together during the weekend for a concert or a baseball game, and the professor would wear his t-shirt and jeans, since he was used to that. But, he noticed that his coworkers dressed up during the weekends. The men would wear nice pants and a button up shirt and the women would wear a fashionable dress with some nice shoes. They wore much nicer clothes than the professor. And so the professor thought that his coworkers dressed classy and sharp. So the professor started to dress more formal. The t-shirt and jeans no longer looked cool to the professor.</u>

Therefore, this is the example the professor uses to explain the concept of <u>reference groups.</u>

Practice 2

Reading Time: 50 seconds

Flagship Species

Human activities constantly threaten the natural habitats of plants and animals. So, environmental groups are constantly working to protect these organisms. One particular way they do this is by choosing a specific organism that represents the threatened habitat to the people. This species is called the flagship species, and most of the time they choose an organism that the people will find attractive and interesting. The purpose of a flagship species is to increase awareness and motivate the people to take part in protecting the threatened environment. Their support of the flagship species ultimately leads to the protection for all the plants and animals living in the threatened habitat.

(CH3-2.mp3)

Using the macaw from the lecture, explain the concept of flagship species.

PREPARATION TIME
00:00:30

RESPONSE TIME
00:00:60

Reading notes:

Title:
Definition or description:
Detail:

Lecture notes:

Lecture's point 1:

Detail:

Lecture's point 2:

Detail:

Response:

Sample response:

The reading passage discusses the concept of flagship species, which is an animal that is selected to be used to raise public awareness and motivate people to take action to protect the threatened habitat. The people's support results in protection for all the plant and animal species living in the threatened area.

In the lecture, the professor gives the example of the macaw. The macaw is a beautiful large sized parrot known for its colorful green, red, and blue feathers. The macaw lives in the South American rainforest where a lot of the trees have been cut down which the macaw relies on for food and nesting. The macaw and the other animals living in the rainforest were in trouble. Other birds, bats, and animals had also lived in the trees. When the trees were cut down, their populations decreased because they had nowhere to live. So, people started to spread the word that the macaw needed help. They made books with information on the macaw and they passed out these brochures to schools and community centers. A lot of people responded by contributing money and helping the group set up protected land where no one could cut down the trees so that the macaw would be safe. Soon, the macaws number increased, and later other animals came back to the forest and their numbers also increased.

Therefore, this is the example the professor uses to explain the concept of flagship species.

Practice 3

Reading Time: 50 seconds

Cultural Lag

In today's modern world, technology changes so quickly, sometimes people have trouble staying in pace with the development. Thus, when new technology surfaces, people have a hard time adapting to the technology. This is called cultural lag, a transition period where people adjust to the technological change. In the beginning, people will have a pessimistic view toward the change since they are not used to the new technology and may not understand it. As time passes, however, their attitudes will come around, and they will incorporate the new technology into their lives successfully.

(CH3-3.mp3)

Using the example of the telephone, explain how it relates to the concept of cultural lag.

PREPARATION TIME
00:00:30

RESPONSE TIME
00:00:60

Reading notes:

Title:

Definition or description:

Detail:

Lecture notes:

Lecture's point 1:

Detail:

Lecture's point 2:

Detail:

Response:

Sample response:

The reading passage discusses the concept of cultural lag, which is when people are struggling for a time to adapt to technological change. At first people will have a negative attitude because they don't understand the new technology, but their attitudes will change once they incorporate the technology into their lives.

In the lecture, the professor gives the example of a telephone. It was an easier and faster way of communication. However, when the telephone became available, only businesses used telephones because they realized that telephones can benefit them in productivity. The general public did not believe that the phones should be used for personal communication. People did not like to listen to someone else without seeing them. Also, they considered rude to call someone instead of visiting them, what they considered as personal connection. However, people gradually changed their minds about the telephone. It took about 30 years, but eventually most homes had telephones. Talking to people without seeing them became more normal. People called one another just to chat for fun. After everyone agreed on certain etiquettes, such as not to call someone late at night, using the telephone no longer became rude.

In conclusion, this is the example the professor uses to explain the concept of cultural lag.

Practice 4

Reading Time: 50 seconds

Epiphytes

In the rainforests of South America, canopies produced by the upper layer of trees can be so dense, that few plants are able to grow on the ground below. Still, plants have adapted to life in these shaded grounds by developing extraordinary ways to survive. For instance, a species of plants called epiphytes use a host plant as a ground for growth. Even though the epiphytes grow on a host tree, they do not absorb any nutrients from the tree. Epiphytes attach themselves 30 or 40 meters above the tree and have access to sunlight, but not nutrients from the ground. So the epiphytes have evolved mechanisms to overcome this obstacle.

(CH3-4.mp3)

Using the example of the urn plant, explain how epiphytes have adapted to life in the rainforest.

PREPARATION TIME
00:00:30

RESPONSE TIME
00:00:60

Reading notes:

Title:

Definition or description:

Detail:

Lecture notes:

Lecture's point 1:

Detail:

Lecture's point 2:

Detail:

Response:

Sample response:

The reading passage discusses the concept of epiphytes, which are plants that use a host plant as a platform for growth. While growing on the tree, the epiphytes do not take any nutrients from it.

In the lecture, the professor gives the example of the urn plant. The urn plant wraps its root around the branches or trunk of the tree. They use the tree for support and this allows them to reside high amongst the trees, where they can get sunlight. The urn plant has a unique shape. Its leaves form a urn or a bowl to store water. The leaves are long and spiky and rolled into a coned shape. The flowers are held in a single stem. When rainwater collects in the leaves, it rolls down into the bowl to be stored. The unique bowl shape helps the plant to gather nutrients. Insects, dead leaves and other debris land on the leaves and are washed down into the stored water, where they are decomposed. The chemical created is nitrogen rich, and the water created is like a liquid fertilizer.

Therefore, this is the example the professor uses to explain the concept of epiphytes.

Practice 5

Reading Time: 50 seconds

Swarm Intelligence

Certain species of insects reside in large groups called swarms. Swarms could number in several thousand insects living together. By being a member of a swarm, insects are able to carry out complex tasks by engaging in complex behaviors. Swarm insects display a complex behavior that is much more advanced than the behavior of an individual insect. This group behavior seen in a swarm is called swarm intelligence. Swarm intelligence results from each insect performing a simple instinctual behavior, which is then repeated by other swarm members that results in a complex behavior. Through this complex behavior, swarms are able to accomplish tasks which would otherwise be impossible for individual insects to achieve.

(CH3-5.mp3)

Explain how the example from the lecture illustrates the concept of swarm intelligence.

PREPARATION TIME
00:00:30

RESPONSE TIME
00:00:60

Reading notes:

Title:
Definition or description:
Detail:

Lecture notes:

Lecture's point 1:

Detail:

Lecture's point 2:

Detail:

Response:

Sample response:

The reading passage discusses the concept of swarm intelligence, which is when each insect performs a simple instinctual behavior that is repeated by another insect and results in a complex behavior. With swarm intelligence, insects are able to accomplish tasks that individual insects would not be able to achieve.

In the lecture, the professor gives the example of ants. Ants live in colonies. They move together to get to a food source. Sometimes the ants may encounter an obstacle. If a group of ants are on a tree branch and looking for food, they may reach the end of the branch. There may be a wide space between the end of the branch they are on and the other branch with the food on it. Alone, these ants will not be able to get to the other side. So what will happen is that one ant will go to the end of the branch and hold onto the branch with its back legs. Then another ant will walk over the first ant, hold onto the first ant with its back legs and stretch out its body. One after another, the other ants will do the same thing until a bridge is formed between the two branches. The connected ants will hold the positions while the other ants cross over and reach the food.

Therefore, this is the example the professor uses to explain the concept of swarm intelligence.

Vocabulary:

commitment	n.	the state or quality of being dedicated to a cause, activity, etc.	*devotion, faithfulness*
attached	adj.	full of affection or fondness.	*fond of, devoted to*
outcome	n.	the way a thing turns out; a consequence.	*result, effect*
assess	v.	evaluate or estimate the nature, ability, or quality of.	*evaluate, judge*
hesitant	adj.	tentative, unsure, or slow in acting or speaking.	*uncertain, doubtful*
determined	adj.	having made a firm decision and being resolved not to change it.	*set on, insistent on*
nag	v.	annoy or irritate (a person) with persistent fault-finding or continuous urging.	*harass, badger*
reference	n.	the action of mentioning or alluding to something.	*mention, quotation*
classy	adj.	stylish and sophisticated.	*stylish, chic*
sharp	adj.	distinct in outline or detail; clearly defined.	*distinct, clear*
threatened	v.	cause (someone or something) to be vulnerable or at risk; endanger.	*endanger, imperil*
ultimately	adv.	finally; in the end.	*eventually, finally*
incorporate	v.	take in or contain (something) as part of a whole; include.	*include, assimilate*
dense	adj.	closely compacted in substance.	*thick, heavy*
overcome	v.	succeed in dealing with (a problem or difficulty).	*prevail, conquer*

obstacle	n.	a thing that blocks one's way or prevents or hinders progress.	*barrier, hurdle*
reside	v.	be situated.	*lie, repose*
decompose	v.	(with reference to a dead body or other organic matter) make or become rotten; decay or cause to decay.	*decay, rot*

Additional vocabulary:

Chapter notes:

CHAPTER
04

Q4 Lecture

Q4 Lecture

Integrated Task

In the last question of the speaking section, you will be listening to a lecture on an academic subject. You are to summarize the lecture for your response. You will have 20 seconds to prepare for your response and 60 seconds to record your answer.

How the question looks like:

Using points and examples from the lecture, discuss how the shark and the dolphin evolved to be successful hunters.

Using points and examples from the talk, explain two advantages of community college.

Using points and examples from the discussion, explain how a low carbohydrate diet might affect an individual's health.

Why do you get a low score on this question?

There are many reasons why test takers will score low on this question.

1) Response that is cut off:

It is important to note that giving an incomplete response, which is when your response is cut off at 60 seconds, will give a lower score. It is better to give a 55 second response with 5 seconds of silence, than a response where you are cut off.

2) Lack of details:

This response is based on how well you can summarize the listening. Be sure to take good notes while listening to the lecture, and mention those details in your response.

3) Information that was not mentioned or phrased incorrectly:

Sometimes, test takers will include information that was not mentioned in the lecture. They tend to do this because they might have background information or personal experience on the matter, or they might have misheard the information. Only include information covered in the listening. Also, information can be said incorrectly. Try your best to understand what was mentioned.

4) Unorganized response:

If there are two points, divide them clearly in your response. Follow the speaking template for this question type.

5) Misuse of grammar:

Surprisingly, grammar is not the biggest aspect that will undermine your score. Remember, most of the students who take the TOEFL test are non-native English speakers, so their grammar will not be perfect. Still, too many grammar mistakes will result in a low score.

6) Speaking too soft or slow:

Your speaking response is graded either by a human or a computer. If your voice is so soft or slow that the computer cannot understand it, you will get a low score even if the content is perfect.

How to answer step-by-step:

1) Listen to the lecture. Take organized notes because the lecture will only be played once.
2) Prepare your response in 20 seconds. During this time, you can organize the notes you took, or practice giving your response.
3) Give your response in 60 seconds.

Notetaking:

It is important to take organized notes, so before you start the speaking section, it is recommended to prepare for your notes. Your notes for this question type should be organized in the following manner:

Main idea:

Lecture's point 1:

Detail:

Lecture's point 2:

Detail:

Listening section:

The lecture will discuss a specific example or topics concerning an academic topic. Most of the time, the lecture will mention two points. Sometimes however, the professor may give a lengthy personal experience supporting a general topic. Regardless, be thorough in taking notes. Even if you have trouble understanding the content, try to write down the words you hear. After all, the point of this question is to summarize, not understand.

The lecture will be under 2 minutes. It is essential that you try to write down as much information as you can. This includes names and numbers, as well as adjectives that were used to describe the object. Remember, the more you summarize, the more points you will get.

An interesting thing to note is that the lecture's main idea is actually stated in the question. So when you are listening to the lecture, there is no need to write the main idea down, just focus on the example or points.

Lecture's main idea examples:

Using points and examples from the lecture, discuss *how the shark and the dolphin evolved to be successful hunters.*
The main idea of the lecture is how the shark and the dolphin evolved to be successful hunters.

Using points and examples from the talk, explain *two advantages of community college.*
The main idea of the lecture explains the two advantages of community college.

Using points and examples from the discussion, explain *how a low carbohydrate diet might affect an individual's health.*
The main idea of the lecture is how a low carbohydrate diet might affect a person's health.

Listen to a lecture in a biology class.

Professor:

Many animals live underneath the soil. These animals include small organisms like worms to bigger mammals. The biggest benefit of living underground is the protection from predators that live above the ground. But, living underground presents its own challenges to the inhabitants. Fortunately, the animals that live underground have adapted physical characteristics to meet the challenges. One of the biggest problems of living underground is moving through the soil. Another problem is protecting the vulnerable parts of the body from the soil as it moves through.

Now, moving through soil is nothing like moving above ground. The soil is thick and dense, so the animals that live underground have evolved features that help them move through the soil more efficiently. For instance, the mole has super wide, strong front feet with long claws to help dig through the dirt. The mole's front feet act like shovels to help move underground. The long claws will dig in to the dirt, loosen it up, and the wide feet will throw the dirt behind and the mole will move forward. The strong wide feet with long claws help the mole to move underground at an unbelievable pace.

Although moving underground can be easy for those animals that live there, small bits of rock and sand can get stuck in the sensitive parts of the animals' body, such as the eyes for mammals. So, the animals have again adapted to prevent this. Let's take the example of the mole again. To start, moles have tiny eyes that are covered by a thin skin, which is a protective membrane with hair on it. The hairs protect the eyes from rocks and sand. As the mole moves through the dirt, with its head in the front, the rocks and sand will come into contact with the hair on the membrane. The particles will then slide off, without getting caught in the membrane. So the mole's eyes are protected this way.

Notetaking:

1) Moving thru soil
x like move above ground
soil = thick + dense
animals evolve to move effic.
EX: mole = super wide front feet + long claw. Help dig
    Feet act like shovels.
    Claws dig, loosen dirt → wide feet throw sand behind → move forward
Move unbelievable pace.

2) Protect vulnerable parts of body from soil
Rocks + sand stuck in sensitive parts. (eyes)
EX: mole = have tiny eyes cover by thin skin. Protective memb. w/ hair.
    Hair protects eyes from sand.
    Move forward, rocks + sand contact with hair → particles slide off
    Eyes protected.

This lecture presents two ideas. This means that in your speaking template, you should divide your response into two points by mentioning the phrases "To begin with" and "Furthermore".

Remember, every detail counts. Your notes should include the characteristics of the soil (thick and dense), description of the mole's front feet (super wide and strong), and how the mole digs through the dirt.

Speaking template:

In the lecture, the professor   Read the main idea from the question.
To begin with,   Point 1 + Details   .
Furthermore,   Point 2 + Details   .
(These / This) (are / is) the (examples / example) the professor uses to explain Read the main idea from the question.

Question:

Using the example of the mole, explain two different types of underground adaptation.

Sample response:

In the lecture, the professor explains two different types of underground adaptation.

To begin with, animals must adapt to moving underground, through the dirt. Moving through the soil is not like moving above the ground since the soil is thick and dense. So animals that live underground have evolved features that help them move through the dirt. For example, the mole has wide and super strong feet with claws. The front feet act like shovels so that it can dig through the dirt. The claws dig and loosen the dirt, then the broad feet throw the dirt behind the mole as the animal moves. These shovel like feet help the mole move through the dirt quickly.

Furthermore, animals must protect the vulnerable parts of their body while moving through the ground. For instance, moles have tiny eyes and they are covered by thin skin, a protective membrane with hair. The hair protects the eyes from dirt particles. So while the mole moves through the dirt, the dirt comes into contact with the hairy membrane. The particles slide by, and the sensitive eye is protected.

Therefore, these are the two different types of underground adaptation.

Practice 1

(CH4-1.mp3)

Using the examples of the Venus flytrap and the sundew, describe two ways that carnivorous plants consume their nutrients.

PREPARATION TIME
00:00:20

RESPONSE TIME
00:00:60

Lecture notes:

Lecture's point 1:

Detail:

Lecture's point 2:

Detail:

Response:

Sample response:

In the lecture, the professor uses the examples of the Venus flytrap and the sundew and describes two ways that carnivorous plants get their nutrients.

To begin with, the professor mentions the active traps. A good example for this is the Venus flytrap. Parts of the plant move to capture its prey. The leaves are special in that they are hinged in the middle. The two halves of the leaves open and close like a mouth to catch insects. On the leaves are sweet nectars that attract the insects. When the insects land on the leaf, they slam shut. Therefore it is an active trap. The leaves close and forms a cage, trapping the insect. The Venus flytrap then digests the insects and gets its nutrients.

Furthermore, the professor mentions that some plants use passive traps, where they do not have moving parts. The professor mentions the sundew plant. They also make a sweet nectar that attracts insects. The leaves are full of little hair that secrete the nectar. When the insects land on the leaves to get the nectar, the hairs on the leaves traps the insects because the hair produces a sticky glue-like substance. So the insects get stuck and cannot escape. The sundew will then digest the insect and absorb the nutrients.

Therefore, these are the examples the professor uses to describe the two ways that carnivorous plants get their nutrients.

Practice 2

(CH4-2.mp3)

Using the examples from the lecture, explain the two types of narrators that an author of fiction may use.

PREPARATION TIME
00:00:20

RESPONSE TIME
00:00:60

Lecture notes:

Lecture's point 1:

Detail:—

Lecture's point 2:

Detail:

Response:

Sample response:

In the lecture, the professor discusses two types of narrators that an author of fiction might use.

To begin with, the professor talks about the objective narrator. The objective narrator will describe the characters in the story, what they do, and what they say but that will be it. For example, if a story shows a man and a woman about to take a trip, the objective narrator will only give the information of what the characters say to each other and what they do. This forces the readers to interpret the events and fill in the information to what the actions and conversations mean.

Another narrator the professor discusses is the omniscient narrator. The narrator here knows everything about the characters. In the same scenario of the man and woman traveling, the readers not only know what the characters are doing and saying, but the readers also know what the characters are thinking. For example, the couple is going to visit a friend of the mans, and the reader knows what the man is thinking, that he is nervous since he hasn't met his friend for a long time and that he is worried if his wife will like the friend. So an omniscient narrator provides more information and will answer questions that the reader might have.

Therefore, these are the two types of narrators that an author of fiction might use.

Practice 3

(CH4-3.mp3)

Using points and examples from the lecture, explain two ways weathering occurs.

PREPARATION TIME
00:00:20

RESPONSE TIME
00:00:60

Lecture notes:

Lecture's point 1:

Detail:

Lecture's point 2:

Detail:

Response:

Sample response:

In the lecture, the professor <u>explains two ways that weathering occurs.</u>

To begin with, <u>rocks are often exposed to water. In cold environments, rocks can be broken by water freezing inside of them. When water freezes, it expands, and over time, this can lead to weathering. If a rock has a small hole or crack in it, rainwater will fall into the crack. Then at night when the temperature drops, the water will freeze. The expanding ice will push the sides of the crack, causing it to get bigger. When this happens repeatedly, the crack will become larger and a piece of the rock will break off.</u>

Furthermore, <u>weathering can also occur by plant growth. If a plant seed gets blown into a rock crack, it will take root inside and the roots will grow into the rock. The plant's roots will cause the rock to break. A good example of this is when a tree is growing on top of rocks. As the tree grows, the tree roots extend into the rock cracks in search of water and nutrients. Over time, the roots grow bigger and wider, causing the cracks to widen and break apart.</u>

In conclusion, <u>these are the two ways that weathering occurs.</u>

Practice 4

(CH4-4.mp3)

Using points and examples from the lecture, explain two ways that a product's container can be designed to appeal to customers.

PREPARATION TIME
00:00:20

RESPONSE TIME
00:00:60

Lecture notes:

Lecture's point 1:

Detail:

Lecture's point 2:

Detail:

Response:

Sample response:

In the lecture, the professor explains two ways that a product's container can be designed to appeal to consumers.

One design goal is to make the container as user friendly as possible. For example, companies began to use plastic containers for condiments, like ketchup, mustard, and mayonnaise. In the past, they were stored in glass containers, where the caps had to be screwed off. Then the ketchup or mustard had to be poured on the food, which would be messy. However, plastic containers were easy to use, so they were more attractive to use. It was much faster and easier than removing a lid.

Another design goal is to make the container with a pleasing appearance, so that consumers can feel comfortable displaying it at home. For instance, a company that sells cookies might sell them in a nice metal box instead of a cardboard box. The metal box will be decorated with nice pictures so that when consumers present the box to their guests, it will look nice and attractive. This will make the product more appealing.

Therefore, these are the two ways that a product's container can be designed to appeal to consumers.

Practice 5

(CH4-5.mp3)

Using the examples from the lecture, explain two developments that allowed ancient Roman cities to expand.

PREPARATION TIME
00:00:20

RESPONSE TIME
00:00:60

Lecture notes:

Lecture's point 1:

Detail:

Lecture's point 2:

Detail:

Response:

Sample response:

In the lecture, the professor explains two developments that allowed ancient Roman cities to expand.

To begin with, the Romans had more advanced technology and so the Romans had advanced building materials. They had a special concrete that would harden under water. This made new kinds of structures possible. Because of the special concrete, the Romans were able to build better bridges. Bridges were able to cross wide rivers and transport materials with wagons and carts. So with these bridges, Roman cities were able to be built on both sides of the rivers.

Furthermore, ancient Romans developed a way to transport fresh clean water. The Romans built aqueducts to transport water to the people. Aqueducts are a series of open channels that transport water from the mountains to the cities. They were carefully planned and built so that a drop in altitude provided a steady flow of water to the cities. The aqueducts moved large amounts of water in great distances and brought fresh water to places far from rivers. So, people had clean water to drink and bathe without being next to a river. And cities were able to grow in new locations.

Therefore, these are the two examples the professor uses to help explain how ancient Roman cities were able to expand.

Vocabulary:

fortunately	adv.	it is fortunate that.	*luckily*
vulnerable	adj.	susceptible to physical or emotional attack or harm.	*endangered, at risk*
evolve	v.	(with reference to an organism or biological feature) develop over successive generations as a result of natural selection.	*develop, progress*
pace	n.	consistent and continuous speed in walking, running, or moving.	*speed, rate*
carnivorous	adj.	(of an animal) feeding on other animals.	*meat-eating*
active	adj.	moving or tending to move about vigorously or frequently.	*alive, lively*
hinged	adj.	attached or joined with a hinge.	
passive	adj.	accepting or allowing what happens or what others do, without active response or resistance.	*submissive, yielding*
secrete	v.	(of a cell, gland, or organ) produce and discharge (a substance).	*produce, discharge*
objective	adj.	(of a person or their judgment) not influenced by personal feelings or opinions in considering and representing facts.	*impartial, unbiased*
omniscient	adj.	knowing everything.	*all-knowing*
exposed	adj.	not covered or hidden; visible.	*unprotected, open*
expand	v.	become or make larger or more extensive.	*enlarge, swell*

extend	v.	cause to cover a larger area; make longer or wider.	*increase, enlarge*
appeal	v.	be attractive or interesting.	*attract, interest*
altitude	n.	great height.	*height, elevation*

Additional vocabulary:

Chapter notes:

Actual Test

01

Speaking Section Directions

In this section of the TOEFL iBT test, you will be asked to demonstrate your ability to speak in English regarding various topics by responding to four questions.

The first question involves a familiar topic. Your response is graded on your ability to speak clearly and logically about the topic.

The next two questions are based on what you have read and heard. First you will read a short text, either a university-related change or an academic topic. Then you will listen to a conversation about the university announcement or a short lecture about the academic topic from the reading. You will then be asked to summarize what you have read and heard. You need to organize and associate information from the text and the talk to provide a complete answer.

In the final question, you will listen to a lecture on an academic topic. You will have to summarize the main points, as well as the details from the lecture. Your response is graded based on how well you can speak clearly and coherently and how well you can summarize the information you have heard.

Throughout the test, you are encouraged to take notes while you read the passage and listen to the talks. Your notes will help you prepare for your response. Listen carefully to the directions for each question because the directions are not written on the screen. You will be given a short time to prepare for each response. A clock will show how much preparation time will remain. When the preparation time is up, you will be told to begin your response. A clock will show how much time you have to respond. A message will appear on the screen when the response time ends.

Actual Test 1

At school, students have to complete various academic assignments. Which one of the assignments below do you think is beneficial for students?

1) Research paper
2) Class presentation
3) Group project

Include examples and details in your response.

PREPARATION TIME
00:00:15

RESPONSE TIME
00:00:45

(AT1-1.mp3)

Notes

Reading Time: 45 seconds

Music Building Open Hours

The campus music building where students can reserve practice rooms to play their instruments closes at nine p.m. every night. However, I believe that the school should open the music building until midnight. Students with instruments often want to practice later at night, but there are no facilities that can accommodate them. Also, many students want to use the practice rooms, but because of limited rooms, it is difficult to reserve one. If the music building were to have longer operation hours, it would be easier for students to reserve the practice rooms.

(AT1-2.mp3)

The woman expresses her opinion about the student's letter to the editor. Explain her opinion and the reasons she gives for holding that opinion.

PREPARATION TIME
00:00:30

RESPONSE TIME
00:00:60

Reading notes:

Announcement:
Detail 1:
Detail 2:

Conversation notes:

Man	Woman
Opinion:	Opinion:
Reason 1:	Reason 1:
Details:	Details:
Reason 2:	Reason 2:
Details:	Details:

Response:

Reading Time: 50 seconds

Refute and Persuade

Often times, companies notice that consumers may have developed a negative impression of their product or service. To solve this issue, companies use an advertising technique known as refute and persuade. This technique involves the advertisement indicating the product's disadvantage, but the company refutes or challenges that drawback by showing the advantage of purchasing and using the product and how it makes up for any problems it may have. Using this method, companies can persuade consumers to buy a product or service, even with its drawbacks.

(AT1-3.mp3)

Using the example from the lecture, explain how it relates to the concept of refute and persuade.

PREPARATION TIME
00:00:30

RESPONSE TIME
00:00:60

Reading notes:

Title:
Definition or description:
Detail:

Lecture notes:

Lecture's point 1:

Detail:

Lecture's point 2:

Detail:

Response:

Actual Test 1

(AT1-4.mp3)

Using the points and examples from the lecture, describe two ways lakes can disappear from nature.

PREPARATION TIME
00:00:20

RESPONSE TIME
00:00:60

Lecture notes:

Lecture's point 1:

Detail:

Lecture's point 2:

Detail:

Response:

Vocabulary:

reserve	v.	arrange for (a room, seat, ticket, etc.) to be kept for the use of a particular person and not given to anyone else.	*book, order*
accommodate	v.	(of physical space, especially a building) provide lodging or sufficient space for.	*board, take in*
limited	adj.	restricted in size, amount, or extent; few, small, or short.	*restricted, finite*
slot	n.	an allotted place in an arrangement or plan such as a broadcasting schedule.	*spot, space*
refute	v.	prove (a statement or theory) to be wrong or false; disprove.	*disprove, rebut*
persuade	v.	cause (someone) to do something through reasoning or argument.	*convince, coax*
impression	n.	an idea, feeling, or opinion about something or someone, especially one formed without conscious thought or on the basis of little evidence.	*feeling, suspicion*
drawback	n.	a feature that renders something less acceptable; a disadvantage or problem.	*downside, catch*
consumers	n.	a person who purchases goods and services for personal use.	*buyer, customer*
warranty	n.	a written guarantee, issued to the purchaser of an article by its manufacturer, promising to repair or replace it if necessary within a specified period of time.	*guarantee, assurance*
permanent	adj.	lasting or intended to last or remain unchanged indefinitely.	*lasting, indefinite*
sediment	n.	matter that settles to the bottom of a liquid; dregs.	*deposit, residue*
decompose	v.	(with reference to a dead body or other organic matter) make or become rotten; decay or cause to decay.	*decay, rot*
irrigate	v.	supply water to (land or crops) to help growth, typically by means of channels.	*water, soak*
external	adj.	belonging to or forming the outer surface or structure of something.	*outside, exterior*

Question 1 Sample response:

I believe that group projects are beneficial for students for the following reasons.

To begin with, group projects allow students to make more friends. For example, when working in a group project, students spend days and weeks working on the assignment. They will have lots of time to chat and become acquainted with one another. Through cooperation, students will establish bonds which will be a stepping ladder towards friendship.

Furthermore, group projects will only give minimal stress to the students. For instance, students are assigned individual parts in a group project. Because the workload has been divided amongst the members, the amount of stress for the project will also have been divided. No single student will have to carry the burden of accomplishing the assignment.

Therefore, I believe that group projects are beneficial for students.

Question 2 Sample response:

The student letter states that the music building should be open till midnight. There are students who wish to practice late at night and also there are limited rooms, so students find it hard to reserve a room to practice in.

In the conversation, the woman agrees with the student letter for the following reasons.

To begin with, she states that it would be wonderful to have a place to practice for longer hours. Right now, students practice in their dorm rooms at night. Even though she tries to keep the volume down, it is still loud. She is afraid her practice will wake up students who are sleeping or bother those who are studying.

Furthermore, the woman states that student can use the extra time slots in the music building. During the concert season, like Winter and Spring, everyone needs to practice. So extending the hours in the music building will benefit the students.

Therefore, these are the reasons why the woman agrees with the student letter.

Question 3 Sample response:

The reading passage discusses the concept of refute and persuade, which is when a company advertises a product's disadvantages but the company refutes any drawbacks by showing the advantages of purchasing and using the product and how it makes up for any problems it may have. This will persuade consumers to buy the product or service, even with its downfalls.

In the lecture, the professor gives his experience of the topic. One day he was watching a television advertisement showing a well-known pots and pans company. A professional chef appeared and commented how she uses the pots and pans in her own kitchen. She mentions the fact that the company's products are expensive and consumers do not intend to spend so much money, especially when there are other pots and pans that cost less. However, the chef explains that the cost is well worth the price because they save money for the consumers in the long run. The company offers a special lifetime warranty, which promises to replace any pots and pans if they were to go wrong. This is actually special since other companies do not offer such lifetime warranty.

Therefore, this is the example the professor uses to explain the concept of refute and persuade.

Question 4 Sample response:

In the lecture, the professor describes two ways lakes can disappear from nature.

To begin with, the lake can become filled with organic sediment. This is seen in lakes with lots of plants. When these plants die, they will fall to the bottom of the lake and decompose. Other plants that have replaced them will also die and fall to the bottom and decompose. Dead plant matter will build up for many years until eventually the lake becomes completely full of dead plant matter.

Furthermore, human activities can make lakes disappear. Farmers will need to irrigate their crops and they will use water from nearby lakes. They will install pipes that connect the lake to the farms so that water can be provided. This irrigation system will be sustainable as long as the lake is refilled by rainwater or incoming stream. However, if there is no external source of water to replace the lake, the lake will eventually dry up.

Therefore, these are the two ways lakes can disappear from nature.

Actual Test
02

Speaking Section Directions

In this section of the TOEFL iBT test, you will be asked to demonstrate your ability to speak in English regarding various topics by responding to four questions.

The first question involves a familiar topic. Your response is graded on your ability to speak clearly and logically about the topic.

The next two questions are based on what you have read and heard. First you will read a short text, either a university-related change or an academic topic. Then you will listen to a conversation about the university announcement or a short lecture about the academic topic from the reading. You will then be asked to summarize what you have read and heard. You need to organize and associate information from the text and the talk to provide a complete answer.

In the final question, you will listen to a lecture on an academic topic. You will have to summarize the main points, as well as the details from the lecture. Your response is graded based on how well you can speak clearly and coherently and how well you can summarize the information you have heard.

Throughout the test, you are encouraged to take notes while you read the passage and listen to the talks. Your notes will help you prepare for your response. Listen carefully to the directions for each question because the directions are not written on the screen. You will be given a short time to prepare for each response. A clock will show how much preparation time will remain. When the preparation time is up, you will be told to begin your response. A clock will show how much time you have to respond. A message will appear on the screen when the response time ends.

Actual Test 2

Some people prefer to study in public places where there are other people around. Others prefer to study in private places where there are few or no people around. Which place do you prefer?

Include specific examples and details in your response.

PREPARATION TIME

00:00:15

RESPONSE TIME

00:00:45

(AT2-1.mp3)

Notes

Actual Test 2

Reading Time: 45 seconds

Removing Old Bicycles from Bicycle Racks

Every time I walked by any campus bicycle rack, I noticed that there were bicycles that had been locked and have not been moved for a long time. The university should remove these bikes from the racks and throw them away. First, the bikes will not be missed, since the owners forgot about the bikes. But more importantly, throwing away these bikes will help free up space on the racks, so that people who are actually using their bikes can have a place to park them.

(AT2-2.mp3)

The woman expresses her opinion about the student's letter to the editor. Explain her opinion and the reasons she gives for holding that opinion.

PREPARATION TIME
00:00:30

RESPONSE TIME
00:00:60

Reading notes:

Announcement:
Detail 1:
Detail 2:

Conversation notes:

Man	Woman
Opinion:	Opinion:
Reason 1:	Reason 1:
Details:	Details:
Reason 2:	Reason 2:
Details:	Details:

Response:

Reading Time: 50 seconds

Scatter Hoarding

In certain environments, food is bountiful during specific times of the year and limited during other times of the year. Many animals live in these kinds of environments. Here, the animals will collect and prepare food during the months it is plentiful and store it for later when there is less food to be found. These hoarders may engage in scatter hoarding. Scatter hoarders are different from other hoarders, in that that they do not store their food in just one place. They will scatter it, by dividing and hiding the food in many different locations. When food is scarce, the hoarders will recover their food from these hiding places.

(AT2-3.mp3)

Using the example from the lecture, explain how it relates to the concept of scatter hoarding.

PREPARATION TIME
00:00:30

RESPONSE TIME
00:00:60

Reading notes:

Title:
Definition or description:
Detail:

Lecture notes:

Lecture's point 1:

Detail:

Lecture's point 2:

Detail:

Response:

Actual Test 2

(AT2-4.mp3)

Using the points and examples from the lecture, explain the two ways a company can diversify.

PREPARATION TIME
00:00:20

RESPONSE TIME
00:00:60

Lecture notes:

Lecture's point 1:

Detail:

Lecture's point 2:

Detail:

Response:

Vocabulary:

public	adj.	of or concerning the people as a whole.	*general, common*
private	adj.	belonging to or for the use of one particular person or group of people only.	*personal, individual*
assumption	n.	a thing that is accepted as true or as certain to happen, without proof.	*supposition, presumption*
rusty	adj.	(of a metal object) affected by rust.	*corroded, tarnished*
forceful	adj.	(especially of a person or argument) strong and assertive; vigorous and powerful.	*assertive, authoritative*
prohibit	v.	formally forbid (something) by law, rule, or other authority.	*forbid, ban*
hardly	adv.	scarcely (used to qualify a statement by saying that it is true to an insignificant degree).	*barely, slightly*
bountiful	adj.	large in quantity; abundant.	*abundant, ample*
engage	v.	participate or become involved in.	*take part in*
hoarder	n.	a person who hoards things.	*collector, saver*
preserve	v.	maintain (something) in its original or existing state.	*conserve, maintain*
potential	adj.	having or showing the capacity to become or develop into something in the future.	*probable, prospective*
diversify	v.	make or become more diverse or varied.	*branch out, expand*
asset	n.	a useful or valuable thing, person, or quality.	*strength, blessing*
likely	adj.	such as well might happen or be true; probable.	*possible, probable*

Question 1 Sample response:

I believe that studying in a private place with few or no people around is better for the following reasons.

To begin with, there is less distraction when you are studying in a reserved space. For example, you are the only person studying within the vicinity, so there will be no distractions from people conversing, walking around, or chatting on their phones. Without such distractions, you will be able to concentrate on your studies.

Furthermore, discreet study environments provide more conveniences to help one study. For instance, nonpublic study rooms have partitions to make sure the person is in their own private area, the lights are fixated on the desk so that it is brightly lit, and there are power sockets on the table to provide people with convenient access to a power source. These amenities provide an excellent environment to study.

Therefore, I believe that studying in a private place with few or no people around is better.

Question 2 Sample response:

The student letter states that the university should remove unused bikes from racks and throw them away. The owners probably forgot about their bikes so they will not be missed. This will help free up space in the bike racks.

In the conversation, the woman agrees with the student letter for the following reasons.

To begin with, she states that it is safe to assume that no one wants the bikes. There are many missing parts, like handle bars and wheels. Also, the bikes are rusty, which probably means they were left out for many years. In the case that the bikes are in use, the school can attach notes on the bikes and give the owner two weeks to remove them, or it will be trashed.

Furthermore, the woman states that the dining hall has so many unused bikes parked in front. So it is hard for her to find an empty space. Plus, students are not allowed to tie their bikes to a post or fence. The woman has to actually park her bike in a different building and walk to the dining hall.

Therefore, these are the reasons why the woman agrees with the student letter.

Question 3 Sample response:

The reading passage discusses the concept of scatter hoarding, which is when animals do not store food in just one place but scatter it, by dividing and hiding the food in many different locations. So when the food is scarce, they can recover the food from the hiding spots.

In the lecture, the professor gives an example of a squirrel that lives in the northeastern part of the United States. Squirrels enjoy eating nuts since it is their primary source of nutrition. During the winter, nuts are hard to find, however they are plentiful in the fall. So the squirrels will gather the nuts in fall and prepare them by taking off the outer shells and cleaning the nut inside. This preparation process actually preserves the nut better and makes it easier to eat later. The squirrels will bury the nuts individually in the ground. There will be hundreds of holes so that even if another animal happens to find a hole, there will be other holes with nuts for the squirrel to enjoy during winter.

Therefore, this is the example the professor uses to explain the concept of scatter hoarding.

Question 4 Sample response:

In the lecture, the professor explains two ways a company can diversify.

The first method is to use an existing technology to make a new product. Since the company already has the machine and technology to make a certain product, they can use the equipment to make a different product. For example, a television company can make computer monitors since they are similar to make. The computer monitors will reach out to new customers, like businesses that need monitors for their workers and not television sets.

The second method is to appeal to existing customers by offering them something they need. Since existing customers are one of the most important assets to a company, the company can provide them with an alternative product. For instance, a ski company can make jackets for their customers who enjoy winter sports. The customers already purchase skis from the company, so they will prefer to buy jackets with the company's name on it.

Therefore, these are the two methods a company can diversify.

Actual Test
03

Speaking Section Directions

In this section of the TOEFL iBT test, you will be asked to demonstrate your ability to speak in English regarding various topics by responding to four questions.

The first question involves a familiar topic. Your response is graded on your ability to speak clearly and logically about the topic.

The next two questions are based on what you have read and heard. First you will read a short text, either a university-related change or an academic topic. Then you will listen to a conversation about the university announcement or a short lecture about the academic topic from the reading. You will then be asked to summarize what you have read and heard. You need to organize and associate information from the text and the talk to provide a complete answer.

In the final question, you will listen to a lecture on an academic topic. You will have to summarize the main points, as well as the details from the lecture. Your response is graded based on how well you can speak clearly and coherently and how well you can summarize the information you have heard.

Throughout the test, you are encouraged to take notes while you read the passage and listen to the talks. Your notes will help you prepare for your response. Listen carefully to the directions for each question because the directions are not written on the screen. You will be given a short time to prepare for each response. A clock will show how much preparation time will remain. When the preparation time is up, you will be told to begin your response. A clock will show how much time you have to respond. A message will appear on the screen when the response time ends.

Actual Test 3

Do you agree or disagree with the following statement? Children require parent's involvement when it comes to choosing a career.

Include specific examples and details in your response.

PREPARATION TIME
00:00:15

RESPONSE TIME
00:00:45

(AT3-1.mp3)

Notes

Reading Time: 45 seconds

Campus Construction

Small construction projects at school, such as fixing sidewalks and parking lots, often occur during the regular school year when students are inside the classrooms. I suggest that when possible, the school should arrange the construction projects to take place during summer vacation. First, these construction projects can be quite disruptive. They may cause inconveniences and make it hard for students to travel around on campus. Also, the construction projects would finish quicker if they were scheduled for the summer, since the weather is usually nice.

(AT3-2.mp3)

The woman expresses her opinion about the student's letter to the editor. Explain her opinion and the reasons she gives for holding that opinion.

PREPARATION TIME
00:00:30

RESPONSE TIME
00:00:60

Reading notes:

Announcement:
Detail 1:
Detail 2:

Conversation notes:

Man	Woman
Opinion:	Opinion:
Reason 1:	Reason 1:
Details:	Details:
Reason 2:	Reason 2:
Details:	Details:

Response:

Reading Time: 50 seconds

Emotional Intelligence

Human intelligence is regarded as the mental ability to analyze and comprehend complex ideas. Many psychologists believe that there is a different type of intelligence, which is called emotional intelligence. Those with emotional intelligence have the ability to recognize their true feelings and come to an understanding of what is causing them. People with emotional intelligence are able to control their emotional responses better, changing or fixing them when necessary. This type of intelligence helps people to behave accordingly in social environments, which help them to maintain good relationships with others.

(AT3-3.mp3)

Using the example from the lecture, explain how it relates to the concept of emotional intelligence.

PREPARATION TIME
00:00:30

RESPONSE TIME
00:00:60

Reading notes:

Title:
Definition or description:
Detail:

Lecture notes:

Lecture's point 1:

Detail:

Lecture's point 2:

Detail:

Response:

Actual Test 3

(AT3-4.mp3)

Using the example of the lizard from the lecture, explain the two benefits of subsurface locomotion.

PREPARATION TIME
00:00:20

RESPONSE TIME
00:00:60

Lecture notes:

Lecture's point 1:

Detail:

Lecture's point 2:

Detail:

Response:

Vocabulary:

involvement	n.	the fact or condition of being involved with or participating in something.	*participation, collaboration*
manage	v.	succeed in surviving or in attaining one's aims, especially against heavy odds; cope.	*cope, make do*
analyze	v.	examine methodically and in detail the constitution or structure of (something, especially information), typically for purposes of explanation and interpretation.	*examine, survey*
mental	adj.	relating to the mind.	*intellectual, cognitive*
uncalled for	adj.	(especially of a person's behavior) undesirable and unnecessary.	*unnecessary, needless*
anxious	adj.	experiencing worry, unease, or nervousness, typically about an imminent event or something with an uncertain outcome.	*apprehensive, uneasy*
subsurface	n.	the stratum or strata below the earth's surface.	
locomotion	n.	movement or the ability to move from one place to another.	*motion, movement*
minimize	v.	reduce (something, especially something unwanted or unpleasant) to the smallest possible amount or degree.	*reduce, decrease*
exposure	n.	the state of being exposed to contact with something.	*vulnerability, subjection*
extreme	adj.	reaching a high or the highest degree; very great.	*greatest, maximum*
via	prep.	by means of.	
origin	n.	the point or place where something begins, arises, or is derived.	*genesis, dawn*

Question 1 Sample response:

I believe that parents should not contribute to deciding their child's career for the following reasons.

To begin with, parents should not have a hand in deciding their child's profession because it can create stress. For example, children are already under stress from deciding which occupation to choose. However, with their parent's input, children will have even more stress due to the nagging that usually follows from a parent's participation. Therefore, parents should not influence a child when they choose their career.

Furthermore, different circumstances prohibit parents from influencing their child's career. For instance, children live in a different era and culture compared to their parents. The trade that was once popular may not be so sought after. So parents should not be involved in their child's decision making process when they choose their future work.

Therefore, I believe that children should not require parent's involvement when it comes to choosing a career.

Question 2 Sample response:

The student letter states that the school should arrange constructions to take place during summer vacations. This is because construction work is disruptive during the school year, which is inconvenient for students when they walk around campus. Also, the construction would finish faster since the weather is nicer during the summer.

In the conversation, the woman agrees with the student letter for the following reasons.

To begin with, she states that she drives to school every day and has difficulty finding a place to park. She remembers last year the school repaired the parking lots and there was not enough space for parking for students and professors. Most times, the woman had to park in the streets, and walk over to the classroom. Her classmates and even her professors were late to class due to parking difficulties.

Furthermore, the woman states that construction last year took longer because of the weather. Last year, there was a snow storm, so the workers had to stop because of the ice and snow. With the continuous pauses, construction took longer to finish.

Therefore, these are the reasons why the woman agrees with the student letter.

Question 3 Sample response:

The reading passage discusses the concept of emotional intelligence, which is the ability to recognize one's true feelings and come to understand its cause. So people with emotional intelligence are better able to control emotional responses by changing or fixing them when necessary.

In the lecture, the professor gives the example of his daughter. When her daughter invited her friend to watch a movie, they argued about which movie to watch. However, it was unlike the daughter for her to get upset about which movie to watch. She stopped arguing and thought why she was so upset. Then she realized that she was upset not because of the movie, but because of a job she would be starting as a summer camp counselor for kids. She was never a counselor so she was worried about her new job and if the kids would like her. After coming to an understanding, the professor's daughter apologized to her friend and told her why she was upset and of the new job. Her friend encouraged her and later they were able to relax and watch a movie together.

Therefore, this is the example the professor uses to explain the concept of emotional intelligence.

Question 4 Sample response:

In the lecture, the professor uses the example of the lizard and explains the two benefits of subsurface locomotion.

The first advantage is decreasing an animal's exposure to extreme temperatures. This is very important for animals that live in extreme environments. For example, a lizard in the Sahara Desert is able to move under the surface very quickly. There is no need for it to go to the surface. So at the same time, the lizard is able to avoid the dangerously high temperatures.

The second advantage is helping predators catch their prey. The prey animals cannot see predators approaching them from underground. For instance, the Sahara Desert lizard is able to sense an insect's vibrations as the insect moves on the ground. The lizard will move underground and go to the origin of the vibration. After approaching the target, it will pop its head to the surface and capture the insect by surprise.

Therefore, these are the two benefits of subsurface locomotion.

Actual Test
04

Speaking Section Directions

In this section of the TOEFL iBT test, you will be asked to demonstrate your ability to speak in English regarding various topics by responding to four questions.

The first question involves a familiar topic. Your response is graded on your ability to speak clearly and logically about the topic.

The next two questions are based on what you have read and heard. First you will read a short text, either a university-related change or an academic topic. Then you will listen to a conversation about the university announcement or a short lecture about the academic topic from the reading. You will then be asked to summarize what you have read and heard. You need to organize and associate information from the text and the talk to provide a complete answer.

In the final question, you will listen to a lecture on an academic topic. You will have to summarize the main points, as well as the details from the lecture. Your response is graded based on how well you can speak clearly and coherently and how well you can summarize the information you have heard.

Throughout the test, you are encouraged to take notes while you read the passage and listen to the talks. Your notes will help you prepare for your response. Listen carefully to the directions for each question because the directions are not written on the screen. You will be given a short time to prepare for each response. A clock will show how much preparation time will remain. When the preparation time is up, you will be told to begin your response. A clock will show how much time you have to respond. A message will appear on the screen when the response time ends.

Actual Test 4

State whether you agree or disagree with the following statement. Explain your reasons using specific details to support your response.

Students should experience working part-time before attending university.

PREPARATION TIME

00:00:15

RESPONSE TIME

00:00:45

(AT4-1.mp3)

Notes

Reading Time: 45 seconds

Library Workspace

Since the time it was built, enormous multiperson study tables have furnished the main campus library. Starting this summer, the large tables will be switched to personal study cubicles, so that individuals can study enclosed by walls in privacy. These new desks will allow students to be isolated and help eliminate noise in the library so that students can concentrate. Also, the cubicles will allow the library to attend to the increase in the number of students. The current study tables seat six students each, and take up too much floor space. On the other hand, the cubicles are designed for maximum space efficiency, and the library will be able to add 50 new seats.

(AT4-2.mp3)

The man expresses his opinion regarding the announcement made by the university. Explain his opinion and the reasons he gives for holding that opinion.

PREPARATION TIME
00:00:30

RESPONSE TIME
00:00:60

Reading notes:

Announcement:
Detail 1.
Detail 2:

Conversation notes:

Man	Woman
Opinion:	Opinion:
Reason 1:	Reason 1:
Details:	Details:
Reason 2:	Reason 2:
Details:	Details:

Response:

Reading Time: 50 seconds

Ritualization

Scientists believe that communicative behavior between animals is developed through a process called ritualization. Ritualization happens when a given behavior changes over time, where a behavior that originally had a practical purpose evolves into something that communicates a specific message. For instance, a specific movement or physical feature might change to serve as a signal or a warning that other animals will come to understand. Once the behavior is ritualized, it becomes a form of communication. So if an animal participates in this behavior, others will interpret the meaning of the act quickly and respond accordingly.

(AT4-3.mp3)

Using the example of dogs discussed in the lecture, explain how it relates to the concept of ritualization.

PREPARATION TIME
00:00:30

RESPONSE TIME
00:00:60

Reading notes:

Title:
Definition or description:
Detail:

Lecture notes:

Lecture's point 1:

Detail:

Lecture's point 2:

Detail:

Response:

Actual Test 4

(AT4-4.mp3)

Using points and examples from the lecture, explain the concept of diffusion.

PREPARATION TIME
00:00:20

RESPONSE TIME
00:00:60

Lecture notes:

Lecture's point 1:

Detail:

Lecture's point 2:

Detail:

Response:

Vocabulary:

furnish	v.	provide (a house or room) with furniture and fittings.	*outfit, embellish*
isolated	adj.	having minimal contact or little in common with others.	*solitary, lonely*
eliminate	v.	completely remove or get rid of (something).	*remove, abolish*
ritual	adj.	(of an action) arising from convention or habit.	*prescribed, formal*
evolve	v.	develop gradually, especially from a simple to a more complex form.	*develop, progress*
accordingly	adv.	in a way that is appropriate to the particular circumstances.	*suitably, appropriately*
threatened	v.	state one's intention to take hostile action against someone in retribution for something done or not done.	*intimidate, menace*
baring	v.	uncover (a part of the body or other thing) and expose it to view.	*uncover, unveil*
realized	v.	become fully aware of (something) as a fact; understand clearly.	*perceive, register*
diffusion	n.	the spreading of something more widely.	*dispersal, scattering*
innovation	n.	the action or process of innovating.	*revolution, change*
philosophy	n.	a theory or attitude held by a person or organization that acts as a guiding principle for behavior.	*belief, ideology*
resist	v.	withstand the action or effect of.	*withstand, counter*
foreign	adj.	strange and unfamiliar.	*unfamiliar, alien*

Question 1 Sample response:

I disagree that students should experience working part-time before attending university for the following reasons.

To begin with, students will receive physical pain from their part-time jobs. For example, since students are not yet college graduates, the only jobs they can do are manual labor jobs. This sort of labor will create stress on the human body and students will suffer from back pains and muscle aches. So students should avoid such pains as much as possible.

Furthermore, students will not have time to work because they should preview their lessons before attending university. For instance, students should preview what they will learn in college because university courses are much more difficult than high school courses. Instead of working, they should be opening their books to study. So students cannot afford time to work part-time.

Therefore, I believe that students should not experience working part-time before attending university.

Question 2 Sample response:

The university announcement states that the library's large tables will be replaced by personal study cubicles so that students can study enclosed by walls in privacy. The cubicles will isolate the students and eliminate unwanted noise. Also, there has been an increase in the number of students, so more students will be able to fit inside the library.

In the conversation, the man disagrees with the university announcement for the following reasons. To begin with, he states that without the multiperson table, students will not be able to meet for group projects. Instead of investing money in cubicles, the university should invest in conference rooms. This will also help reduce the noise.

Furthermore, the man states that there is no problem with overcrowding at the library. He sees empty tables all the time. He thinks it will be a waste of money to replace something that is already efficient for students.

Therefore, these are the reasons why the man disagrees with the university announcement.

Question 3 Sample response:

The reading passage discusses the concept of ritualization, which is when a given behavior changes over time. The behavior originally had a practical purpose but it evolved to communicate a specific message instead. For instance, a specific movement or a physical feature might change to communicate a signal or a warning.

In the lecture, the professor gives an example of a dog. Long ago, the dog would prepare to bite when it was threatened by baring its teeth. It did this to not bite its own lips. Other animals realized that a dog would bare its teeth just before biting. So they saw it as a signal to be careful and to stay away from the dog. As time passed, the dog also realized that just baring the teeth was protection itself. So what began as a preventive measure from biting its own lips changed into a message to warn others. The dog came to an understanding that there was no need to attack, just showing its teeth would deliver the same message.

Therefore, this is the example the professor uses to explain the concept of ritualization.

Question 4 Sample response:

In the lecture, the professor explains the concept of diffusion.

To begin with, cultural items can be adopted from other groups. Diffusion can occur through military conquest, tourism, or television shows. For example, newspaper from the United States is from different cultural sources. Letters and characters were borrowed from a different culture, printing was borrowed from Germany, and paper was borrowed from China. These innovations were shared between cultures and later the United States was able to create the newspaper. So cultural diffusion takes place over long distances and time.

Furthermore, diffusion can be selective. For instance, people in the United States accepted acupuncture, which is an Asian medicine using needles to cure pain. But few understand the philosophy behind it since it is too foreign. When ideas are too different from one's own beliefs and values, then that part of the idea is not accepted. So acupuncture has been diffused into the American minds, but not the philosophy.

Therefore, these are the examples the professor uses to explain the concept of diffusion.

Actual Test
05

Speaking Section Directions

In this section of the TOEFL iBT test, you will be asked to demonstrate your ability to speak in English regarding various topics by responding to four questions.

The first question involves a familiar topic. Your response is graded on your ability to speak clearly and logically about the topic.

The next two questions are based on what you have read and heard. First you will read a short text, either a university-related change or an academic topic. Then you will listen to a conversation about the university announcement or a short lecture about the academic topic from the reading. You will then be asked to summarize what you have read and heard. You need to organize and associate information from the text and the talk to provide a complete answer.

In the final question, you will listen to a lecture on an academic topic. You will have to summarize the main points, as well as the details from the lecture. Your response is graded based on how well you can speak clearly and coherently and how well you can summarize the information you have heard.

Throughout the test, you are encouraged to take notes while you read the passage and listen to the talks. Your notes will help you prepare for your response. Listen carefully to the directions for each question because the directions are not written on the screen. You will be given a short time to prepare for each response. A clock will show how much preparation time will remain. When the preparation time is up, you will be told to begin your response. A clock will show how much time you have to respond. A message will appear on the screen when the response time ends.

Actual Test 5

State whether you agree or disagree with the following statement. Explain your reasons using specific details to support your response.

It is important to learn about other cultures.

PREPARATION TIME
00:00:15

RESPONSE TIME
00:00:45

(AT5-1.mp3)

Notes

Reading Time: 45 seconds

Off-Campus Singing Competitions

Traditionally, the university choir has only given concerts on campus. However, starting next year, the singing ensemble will add competitive events from off-campus to their schedule. The director of the choir believes that competing in singing competitions will increase the quality of the choir's performance because it will motivate students to pursue a higher standard in their abilities. Also, the director hopes that the choir performing outside of school will strengthen the reputation of the school's music program, which will help the program grow.

(AT5-2.mp3)

The man expresses his opinion regarding the announcement made by the university. Explain his opinion and the reasons he gives for holding that opinion.

PREPARATION TIME
00:00:30

RESPONSE TIME
00:00:60

Reading notes:

Announcement:

Detail 1:

Detail 2:

Conversation notes:

Man	Woman
Opinion:	Opinion:
Reason 1:	Reason 1:
Details:	Details:
Reason 2:	Reason 2:
Details:	Details:

Response:

Actual Test 5

Reading Time: 50 seconds

Relict Behavior

In most scenarios, animals behave in ways that will help them survive in their natural habitats. However, an animal may sometimes display a behavior that seems to hold no clear purpose. The behavior's original purpose may have lost its function a long time ago. These behaviors are called relict behaviors and were at one time useful to the animal when their habitat was different. With the changing of condition however, the behavior does not serve its intended purpose. Thus, the behavior that was influenced by environmental changes has become a relict.

(AT5-3.mp3)

Using the example of the pronghorn and lion, explain the concept of a relict behavior.

PREPARATION TIME
00:00:30

RESPONSE TIME
00:00:60

Reading notes:

Title:
Definition or description:
Detail:

Lecture notes:

Lecture's point 1:

Detail:

Lecture's point 2:

Detail:

Response:

Actual Test 5

(AT5-4.mp3)

Using points and examples from the lecture, explain how the characteristics of target customers influence marketing strategy for products.

PREPARATION TIME
00:00:20

RESPONSE TIME
00:00:60

Lecture notes:

Lecture's point 1:

Detail:

Lecture's point 2:

Detail:

Response:

Vocabulary:

tradition	n.	a long-established custom or belief that has been passed on from one generation to another.	*custom, practice*
ensemble	n.	a group of musicians, actors, or dancers who perform together.	*group, band*
reputation	n.	a widespread belief that someone or something has a particular habit or characteristic.	*status, standing*
recruit	v.	enroll (someone) as a member or worker in an organization or as a supporter of a cause.	*enroll, sign up*
relict	n.	a thing which has survived from an earlier period or in a primitive form.	
intended	adj.	planned or meant.	*intentional, deliberate*
notable	adj.	worthy of attention or notice; remarkable.	*remarkable, outstanding*
swift	adj.	happening quickly or promptly.	*prompt, instant*
prone	adj.	likely to or liable to suffer from, do, or experience something, typically something regrettable or unwelcome.	*inclined, subject*

Question 1 Sample response:

I disagree that it is important to learn other cultures for the following reasons.

To begin with, people will learn incorrectly when they try to learn other cultures. For example, people are exposed to different cultures by different forms of media, usually movies and music. The media twists information to make the movie or music more appealing, so people are exposed to misleading cultural facts. So it is better not to learn other cultures.

Furthermore, it will take too much time to learn other cultures. For instance, a culture is composed of different parts, with language being the center. Just learning a new language may take years. Aside from language, one must learn the cuisines, mannerism, history, and more just to be familiar with that culture. It would take too much time away from individuals, who are already busy with their studies or work to learn another culture.

Therefore, I believe that it is not important to learn other cultures.

Question 2 Sample response:

The university announcement states that the university choir will add competitive events from off-campus to their schedule. This will increase the quality of the choir's performance and strengthen the reputation of the school's music program.

In the conversation, the man agrees with the university announcement for the following reasons. To begin with, he states that it will help motivate students. Other schools are really good at singing, so students will have to work hard to compete with them. Right now, they only practice once a week. If they practice more, the students will be able to improve their skills.

Furthermore, the man states that the music program will be improved. Right now, the music program is small. Performing off-campus will recruit more talents to the music program because people will hear how good they are and it will attract students to attend the university and join the choir group.

Therefore, these are the reasons why the man agrees with the university announcement.

Question 3 Sample response:

The reading passage discusses the concept of relict behavior, which is when a behavior's original purpose lost its function a long time ago. The changing conditions the animal lives in, such as the environment, may alter its behavior since it does not serve its intended purpose.

In the lecture, the professor gives an example of the American Pronghorn, which lives in North America. They are deer-like animals that live in the grassy plains. Pronghorns are really fast, actually they are the fastest animals in the western hemisphere. Its predators, like the bobcat and coyote, cannot keep up with its speed. The Pronghorn became fast runners because long ago, lions used to hunt the Pronghorn. Lions are swift runners, faster than the bobcat and coyote. So the Pronghorn also had to be quick to survive. When the lions became extinct in the region, it no longer endangered the Pronghorn and they remained faster than ever.

Therefore, this is the example the professor uses to explain the concept of relict behavior.

Question 4 Sample response:

In the lecture, the professor explains how the characteristics of target customers influence marketing strategy for products.

The first characteristic is when a toy company wants to sell toy cars. Their target customers will be kids, so they will advertise during the times kids watch television. This way, the company's target customers will be watching their advertisements and the kids will buy the toy cars themselves or ask their parents to buy it for them.

The second characteristic is geographic location. If a boat company wants to sell boats, their target customers would have to reside near oceans and lakes so that they can ride the boats. The company will therefore advertise along roads or on television in cities located next to oceans and lakes. This will increase their chances of reaching out to their target customers and sell more boats.

Therefore, these are the two characteristics of target customers influencing market strategy for products.

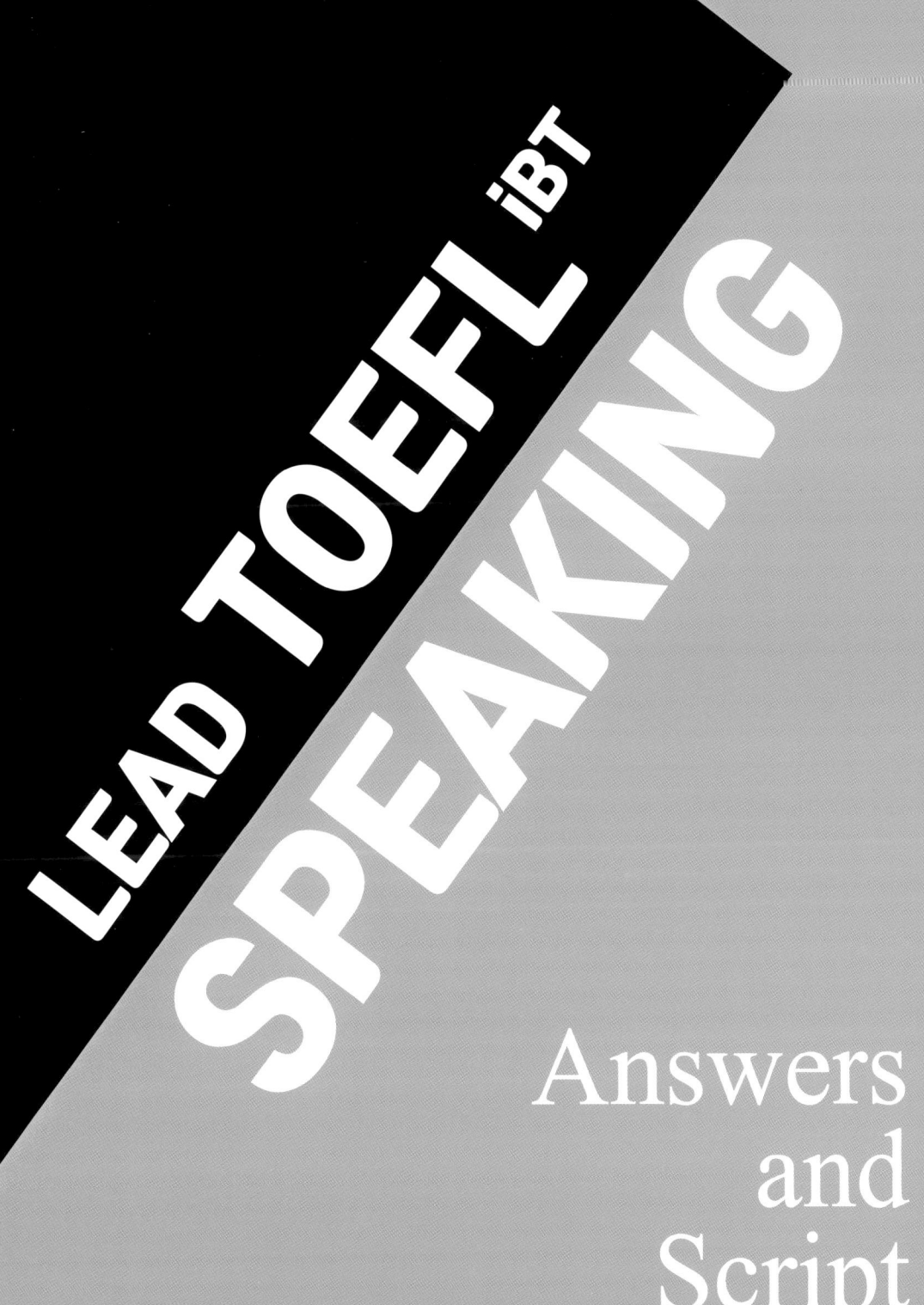

LEAD TOEFL iBT SPEAKING

Answers
and
Script

Answers
and
Script

Chapter01
Q1 Preference

Q1. 선호

이 과제는 당신의 선호도, 경험, 지식을 바탕으로 질문에 답할 것을 요구한다. 옳고 그름은 없다. 그러나 당신의 생각을 뒷받침하는 세부 사항과 함께 논리적으로 제시해야 한다. 응답 준비 시간은 15초, 답변을 녹음하는 시간은 45초 이다.

문제가 어떻게 제시되는가?

일부 사람들은 손 편지를 보내 연락하는 것을 선호한다. 다른 이들은 전화를 이용하여 의사소통 하는 것을 선호한다. 당신이 선호하는 방식은 무엇이며 그 이유는 무엇인가?

아래에 제시된 진술에 대해 동의하는지 반대하는지 말하시오. 구체적인 세부 사항과 예시를 들어 당신의 답변을 말하시오.
자신의 경험을 통해 배우는 것이 다른 사람의 충고로 배우는 것보다 낫다.

당신은 컴퓨터 게임이 아이들에게 부정적인 영향을 미친다고 생각하는가, 아니면 긍정적인 영향을 미친다고 생각하는가? 예시와 세부 사항을 응답에 포함시키시오.

다음 중 어떤 여행을 더 좋아하는가?
오랫동안 당신의 고향 근처에서 여행하기
짧은 기간 동안 당신의 고향 멀리에서 여행하기

왜 이 문제에서 낮은 점수를 받는가?

수험생들이 이 문제에서 낮은 점수를 받는 데는 여러 가지 이유가 있다.

1) **45초 모두 사용하지 않는다.** 이 질문은 대답하기 위해 45초를 준다. 45초 내내 말을 할 수 있도록 대답을 정리해야 한다.

2) **잘린 답변.** 45초 만에 응답이 끊기는 불완전한 응답을 하는 것도 점수가 낮아진다는 점에도 유의해야 한다. 잘린 답변보다 40초간 응답하고 5초간 침묵하는 것이 좋다.

3) **질문을 잘못 읽음.** 때로는 "NOT"와 같은 한 단어가 전혀 다른 응답을 이끌어낼 수 있다. 토플 시험은 단어 몇 개를 바꾸어서 그들의 문제를 간단히 바꾼다.

4) **비논리적 대답.** 답변은 일관성과 논리가 있어야 한다. 그냥 우물쭈물하거나 엉뚱한 대답을 해선 안 된다. 이유, 설명, 예시가 연결되어 있고 잘 정리되어 있는지 확인하라.

5) **설득력 없음.** 당신의 선호에 대한 두 가지 좋은 이유를 언급하더라도, 뒷받침할 예시나 설명이 없다면 낮은 점수를 받게 된다.

6) **문법 오용.** 놀랍게도, 문법은 점수를 감점시키는 가장 큰 측면은 아니다. 기억하라, 토플 시험을 보는 대부분의 학생들은 원어민이 아닌 영어 사용자들이기 때문에 그들의 문법은 완벽하지 않을 것이다. 그래도 문법 실수가 너무 많으면 점수가 낮아진다.

7) **말이 너무 부드럽거나 느리다.** 스피킹 답변은 사람 또는 컴퓨터에 의해 등급이 매겨진다. 목소리가 너무 부드럽거나 느려서 컴퓨터가 알아듣지 못하면 내용이 완벽해도 낮은 점수를 받는다.

Page.14~15

단계별 답변 방법

1) 질문을 주의 깊게 읽어라
2) 질문이 무엇을 요구하는지 확인하라
3) 15초의 준비 시간 동안 당신의 아이디어를 조직하라
4) 45초 이내에 답변하라

준비 시간

15초 동안 답변을 준비할 수 있다. 사실은 30초 가까이 답변을 준비할 시간이 있다. 왜냐하면 토플 시험의 모든 것이 자동화되어 있기 때문인데, 이는 컴퓨터가 당신을 위해 문제를 읽어 줄 것이라는 것을 의미하기도 한다. 그러나 눈으로 질문을 읽는 것은 컴퓨터가 읽어주는 것보다 훨씬 빠르기 때문에 컴퓨터가 여전히 큰 소리로 질문을 읽고 있는 동안, 여러분은 먼저 대답을 준비하기 시작할 수 있다. 컴퓨터가 문제를 다 읽고 나면 수험생에게 15초 동안 답변을 준비할 수 있는 시간을 주겠다고 알린다. 하지만 똑똑한 수험생은 이미 이 시간에 답변을 준비하고 있다.

준비 시간에는 준비할 수 있는 것이 많지 않다. 당신의 개요는 다음과 같아야 한다.

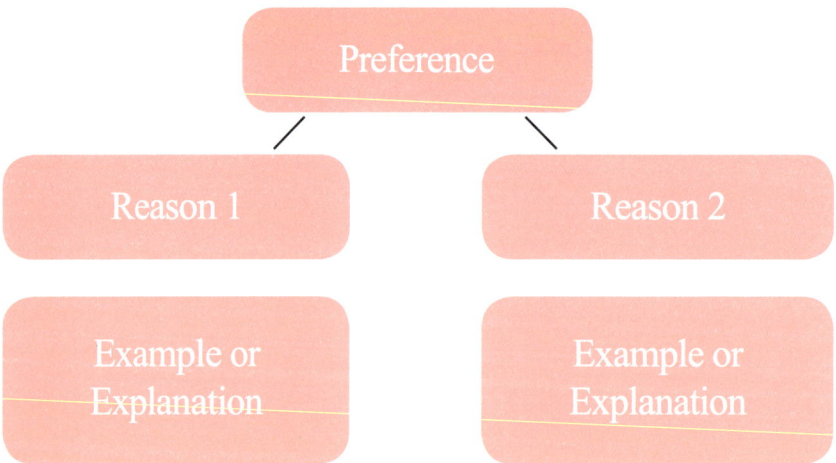

대부분의 수험생들이 솔직한 답변을 하겠지만, 객관적인 답변이 더 수월할 것이라는 점을 명심해야 한다.
아래 표에는 이 질문 유형에서 가장 일반적으로 사용되는 몇 가지 이유가 나열되어 있다.

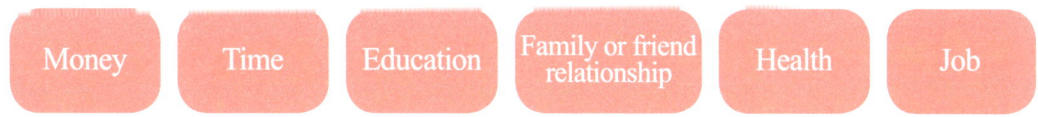

스피킹 템플릿

토플 스피킹 답변은 무심코 말해서는 안 된다. 당신의 답변은 명확하고 이해하기 쉽도록 정리되어야 한다.

아래는 답변 예시이다.

위의 양식에 있는 단어 그대로 따라 써서는 안 된다. 당신의 답변을 위해 사용할 수 있는 다른 표현들이 있다.

Page.16

예시 질문과 답변

Q. 당신은 컴퓨터 게임이 아이들에게 부정적인 영향을 미친다고 생각하는가, 아니면 긍정적인 영향을 미친다고 생각하는가? 예시와 세부 사항을 답변에 포함시켜라.

나는 다음과 같은 이유로 컴퓨터 게임이 아이들에게 긍정적인 영향을 준다고 믿는다.

우선, 컴퓨터 게임은 아이들이 스트레스를 푸는 것을 도울 것이다. 구체적으로 말하면, 아이들은 어린 나이에 공부를 시작한다. 그들은 높은 점수를 얻고 좋은 성적을 유지하기 위해 열심히 공부하기 때문에 공부로부터 스트레스를 받는다. 이러한 스트레스는 컴퓨터 게임을 함으로써 풀 수 있는데, 이러한 게임의 목적은 플레이어의 일상 생활에서 즐거움을 주고 스트레스를 풀게 하는 데 있기 때문이다.

게다가, 아이들은 컴퓨터 게임을 함으로써 더 많은 친구들을 사귈 수 있을 것이다. 예를 들어, 전 세계의 많은 플레이어들이 컴퓨터 게임을 하기 위해 온라인에서 만난다. 게임 중에 서로 수다를 떨게 되고 그 과정에서 우정이 형성될 수 있다. 이것은 아이들의 친구 관계를 확장 시킬 것이다.

그러므로, 이는 컴퓨터 게임이 아이들에게 긍정적인 영향을 미치는 이유들이다.

연습1

Question 1 of 4

당신은 다음의 말에 동의하는가 또는 동의하지 않는가?
학생들이 교실에 핸드폰을 가져오는 것은 허용되어야 한다.
답변에 예시와 세부 사항을 포함시키시오.

예시 답안 :

나는 다음과 같은 이유로 학생들이 교실에 핸드폰을 가지고 들어오는 것이 허용되어야 한다고 생각한다.

우선, 학생들은 가족의 비상 상황에 대비하여 근처에 휴대폰을 소지하고 있어야 한다. 예를 들어, 할머니가 죽음에 임박해 있는데, 마침 전화기를 가지고 있다면, 사랑하는 할머니와 마지막 대화를 나눌 수 있을 것이다. 만약 당신이 교실에서 핸드폰을 소지하지 않았다면, 이것은 불가능했을 것이다.

게다가, 학생들은 정부가 휴대폰을 통해 보내는 경보로 건강을 유지할 수 있다. 예를 들어, 코로나19 유행병으로 인해, 정부는 끊임없이 시민들에게 손을 씻고 사회적 거리를 둘 것을 상기시킨다. 수업 시간에 휴대폰을 가지고 있으면 당신이 손을 씻고 건강을 유지해야 한다는 것을 항상 기억할 수 있을 것이다.

따라서, 이러한 이유로 학생들은 교실에 휴대폰을 가지고 들어갈 수 있어야 한다.

Page.19~20

연습2

Question 1 of 4
다른 문화에 대해 배우는것 혹은 완전히 무시하는 어느 것이 중요한가? 예시와 세부 사항을 답변에 포함시키시오.

예시 답안 :

나는 다음과 같은 이유로 다른 문화에 대해 배우는 것이 중요하다고 생각한다.
우선, 친구들의 네트워크가 커질 것이다. 예를 들어, 우리는 글로벌 사회에 살고 있다. 당신의 동네에 외국인들이 돌아다니는 것은 흔히 볼 수 있는 광경이다. 만약 당신이 그들의 문화에 대해 배운다면, 그들과 친구가 되는 것이 쉬울 것이고 친구들의 네트워크는 커질 것이다. 결국 친구가 많을수록 좋다.

게다가, 당신은 여행할 때 스트레스를 덜 받을 것이다. 예를 들어, 언어와 예절과 같은 다른 문화에 익숙해짐으로써, 당신은 여행할 때 스트레스를 받지 않을 것이다. 나는 작년에 스페인에 갔었고, 언어와 예절을 잘 몰랐다. 그래서 내가 무엇을 할지 몰랐기 때문에 여행 중에 계속 스트레스를 받았다.

그러므로, 이러한 것들이 다른 문화에 대해 배워야 하는 중요한 이유이다.

연습3

Question 1 of 4

당신은 팀원들에게 어떤 자질이 중요하다고 생각하는가?
  1) **리더십**
  2) **협동심**
  3) **인내심**

예시와 세부 사항을 답변에 포함시키시오.

예시 답안 :

내가 생각하기에 팀원에게 중요한 자질은 리더십인데, 그 이유는 다음과 같다.

우선, 리더십 있는 사람이 있다면 팀 내 스트레스 수준이 낮아질 것이다. 예를 들어, 리더는 팀원들이 당면한 프로젝트에 대해 걱정하지 않게끔 지시하면서 적절한 방향으로 팀을 이끌 것이다. 따라서, 팀이 경험하는 스트레스 수준은 감소할 것이다.

나아가 리더십이 있는 사람이 있으면 귀한 같은 시간을 절약할 수 있을 것이다. 예를 들어, 대부분의 경우, 팀원들끼리 논쟁하기도 하고, 과제를 완료하느라 시간을 연장한다. 그러나 리더가 각 개인에게 과제를 부여한다면, 논쟁은 없을 것이고 팀은 시간을 낭비하지 않고 프로젝트를 진행할 수 있을 것이다.

그러므로 나는 누군가를 팀의 소중한 일원으로 만드는 자질이 바로 리더십이라고 믿는다.

연습4

> **Question 1 of 4**
>
> 어떤 사람들은 텔레비전 뉴스를 통해 시사 문제들을 접하는 것을 선호한다. 또 어떤 사람들은 신문을 읽음으로써 뉴스를 접하는 것을 선호한다. 당신은 어떤 방법을 선호하는가?
> 예시와 세부 사항을 답변에 포함시키시오.

예시 답변 :

> 나는 다음과 같은 이유로 텔레비전 뉴스를 통해 시사 문제 배우기를 선호한다.
> 우선, 이것은 시간을 낭비하지 않을 것이다. 예를 들어, 학생으로서 내 시간의 대부분은 과제나 공부에 사용된다. 그래서 텔레비전 뉴스는 내가 숙제를 하는 동안 뉴스 앵커가 뉴스를 들려주기 때문에 내 시간을 절약하는 데 도움이 될 것이다. 만약 내가 직접 신문을 읽어야 한다면, 읽는 데 시간이 걸리기 때문에 시간을 절약하는 것은 불가능할 것이다.
> 게다가, 텔레비전 뉴스는 나에게 필수적인 정보만을 제공할 것이다. 예를 들어, 뉴스 앵커들은 뉴스의 하이라이트와 주요 세부 사항만을 읽을 것이다. 신문들은 그다지 중요하지 않을 수도 있는 모든 세부 사항들을 적는 경향이 있다. 그러나 텔레비전 뉴스는 간략한 요지만을 제공할 것이다.
> 그러므로 이러한 것들이 내가 시사 문제에 뒤떨어지지 않도록 텔레비전 뉴스를 시청하는 것을 더욱 선호하는 이유다.

연습5

Question 1 of 4
당신은 다음 진술에 동의하는가, 동의하지 않는가? **친구는 한 사람의 인생에서 가장 중요한 영향을 끼친다.** 예시와 세부 사항을 답변에 포함시키시오.

예시 답변 :

나는 다음과 같은 이유로 친구가 내 인생에서 가장 중요한 영향을 미친다는 것에 동의한다. 우선, 나는 친구들과 가장 많은 시간을 보낸다. 나는 일주일 중 5일을 친구들과 학교에 같이 가고, 학원에서도 함께 공부를 하며 시간을 보내고, 주말에도 같이 어울린다. 수많은 시간을 함께 보내기 때문에 친구들의 영향을 받는 것은 불가피하다.

게다가, 우리가 비슷한 상황에 있기 때문에 나는 친구들로부터 영향을 받는다. 예를 들어, 학생으로서, 우리는 성적 유지에 대한 부담을 공유한다. 청소년으로서 우리는 비슷한 취미와 관심사를 공유하고 있다. 비슷한 배경 때문에 친구들끼리 서로를 이해하고 서로에게 더 많은 영향을 줄 것이다.

그러므로, 이러한 것들이 친구가 내 인생에 가장 중요한 영향을 미친다고 믿는 이유들이다.

연습6

Question 1 of 4

일부 사람들은 대학들이 전체 성적 평균을 기준으로 학생들을 받아들여야 한다고 생각한다. 다른 사람들은 학교가 그들의 교육 과정 외의 활동에 근거하여 학생들을 받아들여야 한다고 믿는다. 당신은 어느 것을 더 선호하는가?
예시와 세부 사항을 답변에 포함시키시오.

예시 답변 :

나는 다음과 같은 이유로 대학들이 전체 성적 평균을 기준으로 학생들을 받아들여야 한다고 생각한다.

우선, 더 높은 학점 평균은 대학에서 더 나은 결과를 보여줄 것이다. 결국 고등 교육에 입학하는 목적은 졸업 후에 좋은 직업을 보장 받기 위함이다. 이것은 좋은 성적을 받아야만 가능할 것이다. 그래서 성적 평균이 높은 학생은 이것을 성취할 가능성이 더 높을 것이다.

게다가, 대학들은 학교의 이미지를 홍보할 것이기 때문에 전체 성적 평균을 기준으로 학생들을 받아들여야 한다. 예를 들어, 하버드나 예일과 같은 학교들이 상위 계층의 학교들로 간주되는 이유가 있다: 그들은 교육 면에서 뛰어나고 똑똑한 학생들을 지속적으로 보유한다. 학교가 이러한 유명한 이미지를 가지거나 지속하기 위해서, 그들은 반드시 학생들의 성적을 고려해야 한다.

따라서, 나는 대학들이 전체 성적 평균을 기준으로 학생들을 받아들여야 한다고 생각한다.

연습7

<table>
<tr><td align="center">**Question 1 of 4**</td></tr>
<tr><td>어떤 사람들은 그들의 자유 시간을 독서, 생각, 혹은 글쓰기 같은 활동을 하면서 보낸다. 다른 이들은 스포츠와 같은 단체 활동에 참여하면서 사람들과 자유 시간을 보낸다.
당신은 어느 것이 더 좋다고 생각하는가?
예시와 세부 사항을 답변에 포함시키시오.</td></tr>
</table>

예시 답변 :

나는 다음과 같은 이유로 혼자 독서, 생각, 글쓰기 등의 활동을 하며 여가 시간을 보내는 것을 선호한다.

우선 혼자 시간을 보내는 것이 비용 면에서 더 효율적이다. 예를 들어 책을 읽는 것과 같은 독립적인 활동은 책만 필요로 하는데, 그것은 지역 도서관에서 무료로 빌릴 수 있다. 그러나 스포츠와 같은 단체 활동은 장비를 구입하거나 빌리는 것뿐만 아니라, 경기장을 빌리는 데도 돈이 필요하다. 또한, 스포츠를 한 후에 사람들은 보통 함께 외식을 하러 나가는데, 이것은 더 많은 돈이 들 수 있다.

게다가, 혼자 시간을 보내는 것은 스트레스를 덜 수반한다. 예를 들어, 당신이 혼자 무언가를 할 때, 다른 사람의 스케줄이나 선호도에 맞출 필요가 없다. 그러나 단체 활동에서는 모든 사람이 같은 시간에 만나야 하고, 같은 활동에 모두 동의해야 한다. 이것은 불필요한 스트레스가 생기는 논쟁으로 이어질 수 있다.

따라서 다른 사람들과 함께 시간을 보내는 것보다 혼자 시간을 보내는 것이 더 효율적이다.

Page.31~32

연습8

Question 1 of 4

당신은 다음의 말에 동의하는가 동의하지 않는가?
학생들은 소규모 수업보다 더 많은 학생들이 있는 수업에서 유익을 얻는다.
예시와 세부 사항을 답변에 포함시키시오.

예시 답변 :

나는 다음과 같은 이유로 학생들이 소규모 수업보다 다수의 학생들이 있는 수업에서 유익을 얻는다는 것에 동의한다.

우선, 학생들은 새로운 친구들을 사귈 수 있는 더 많은 기회를 가질 것이다. 예를 들어 학교는 공부만 하는 곳이 아니라 좋은 친구를 사귀는 곳이다. 많은 수의 학생들이 있는 교실에 있기 때문에, 그들은 서로 다른 배경을 가진 친구들을 사귈 수 있는 더 많은 기회를 갖게 될 것이다.

게다가, 더 많은 학생들과 함께 교실에 있는 것은 공유할 수 있는 많은 아이디어들을 만들어 낼 것이다. 예를 들어, 유명한 속담에 따르면, "두 개의 머리가 한 개보다 낫다"고 하는데, 더 많은 학생들이 서로 다른 배경에서 왔고 공유할 수 있는 다양한 경험을 가지고 있기 때문에 더 많은 아이디어를 나눌 수 있다.

그러므로, 이것이 다수의 학생들이 교실에 있는 것이 이로운 이유다.

연습9

<table>
<tr><td colspan="1" align="center">Question 1 of 4</td></tr>
<tr><td>

당신은 다음의 말에 동의하는가 또는 동의하지 않는가?
책을 읽는 것이 배우는 데 있어서 가장 좋은 방법이다.
예시와 세부 사항을 답변에 포함시키시오.

</td></tr>
</table>

예시 답변 :

나는 다음과 같은 이유로 책을 읽는 것이 배우는 데 가장 좋은 방법이라는 것에 동의하지 않는다.

우선, 책은 매우 비쌀 수 있다. 예를 들어, 대학의 전형적인 과학 서적은 100달러 이상이다. 학생으로서, 그들은 그렇게 비싼 책을 살 수 있을 만큼 수입이 많지 않을 것이다. 유명 교수들이 무료로 진행하는 온라인 강의처럼 비용 면에서 더 효율적인 학습 방법들이 있다.

게다가, 책을 읽고 배우는 것은 너무 많은 집중력이 드는데, 대부분의 학생들은 집중력이 부족하다. 예를 들어, 책을 읽는 것은 독해하고 이해하는 데 몇 시간이 걸릴 수 있다. 그러나 학생들은 밖에서 놀거나 친구들과 어울리기 때문에 보통 이런 집중력이 부족하다.

오히려 실질적인 경험이 학생들을 공부에 참여시키고, 그들은 수업에 온전히 집중할 수 있다.

따라서 이것들이 책을 읽는 것이 가장 좋은 학습 방법이 아닌 이유들이다.

Page.35~36

연습10

Question 1 of 4

당신은 매번 물건을 보관하고 수집하는 것을 선호하는가, 아니면 버리고 새로운 물건을 구입하는 것을 선호하는가?
예시와 세부 사항을 답변에 포함시키시오.

예시 답변 :

나는 다음과 같은 이유로 물건을 보관하고 모으는 것을 선호한다.
우선, 물건을 보관하고 모으는 것은 돈을 절약할 것이고 때로는 이익을 낼 것이다. 예를 들어, 많은 사람들이 오래된 장난감을 버리지만, 이 장난감들은 자선 단체나 동생에게 줄 수 있기 때문에, 받는 사람들은 장난감 값을 지불할 필요가 없을 것이다. 또 어떤 장난감은 해가 갈수록 가치가 높아지기 때문에 몇 년이 지난 후에 주인은 원래 가치의 두 세 배를 벌 수 있다.
게다가, 나는 감성적인 이유로 물건을 보관하고 모으는 것을 더 좋아한다. 예를 들어, 내가 가지고 있는 많은 기억들은 물건에 저장된다. 옛날 레코드를 들을 때 아내와 함께 처음 노래를 들었던 기억이 난다. 또는 오래되고 낡은 아이의 구두를 보면 아들이 첫 발을 내디딘 기억이 난다
그러므로 이것들이 내가 물건을 보관하고 모으는 이유이다.

Chapter02
Q1 Announcement and Opinion

Page.40

Q2. 공고와 의견

이 문제 유형에서 당신은 학생의 편지나 대학의 발표, 문제에 대한 학생의 의견을 요약해야 한다. 주요 아이디어를 얼마나 잘 요약할 수 있는지, 리딩와 리스닝에 언급된 내용을 바탕으로 점수가 주어진다. 답변을 준비할 시간은 30초, 답변을 녹음할 시간은 60초가 주어진다.

문제는 어떻게 제시되는가:

> 여자는 대학의 발표에 대해 자신의 의견을 말한다. 그녀의 의견과 그 의견을 지지하는 이유를 진술하라.

> 여자는 새 기숙사에 대한 발표에 대해 의견을 표명한다. 그녀의 의견을 서술하고 그 의견을 지지하는 이유를 설명하라.

> 남자가 학생의 편지에 대해 자신의 의견을 말한다. 그의 의견을 서술하고 그 의견을 지지하는 이유를 설명하라.

Page.41

왜 이 문항에서 낮은 점수를 받는가?

수험생들이 이 문제에서 낮은 점수를 받는 데는 여러 가지 이유가 있다.

1) **잘린 응답.** 60초에서 응답이 끊기는 불완전한 응답을 하면 더 낮은 점수를 받는다는 것에 유의해야 한다. 단절된 응답보다는 55초간 답변을 하고, 5초 정도 침묵하는 것이 좋다.

2) **다른 사람의 의견 요약하기.** 매우 드물게, 수험자들은 다른 사람의 의견을 요약할 것이다. 문제에 알맞은 사람을 요약하고 있는지 확인하라.

3) **세부사항 부족.** 이 답변은 리딩과 리스닝을 얼마나 잘 요약할 수 있느냐에 기초한다. 리딩을 읽고 대화를 들을 때는 반드시 잘 메모하고, 답변에 그 세부 사항을 언급하라.

4) **언급되지 않은 정보.** 때때로 수험생들은 리딩과 리스닝에 언급되지 않은 정보를 포함시킨다. 그들은 이 문제에 관한 배경 지식 혹은 개인적인 경험을 가지고 있거나, 정보를 잘못 들었을 수도 있기 때문에 이렇게 하는 경향이 있다. 리딩 및 리스닝에서 언급된 정보만 포함하라

5) **조직되지 않은 답변.** 리딩의 요약이 먼저 제시되고, 그 다음에 리스닝이 나와야 한다. 이 질문 유형의 말하기 템플릿을 따르라.

6) **문법 오용.** 놀랍게도, 문법은 점수를 감점시키는 가장 큰 측면은 아니다. 기억하라, 토플 시험을 보는 대부분의 학생들은 원어민이 아닌 영어 사용자들이기 때문에 그들의 문법이 완벽하지 않을 것이다. 그래도 문법 실수가 너무 많으면 점수가 낮아진다.

7) **말이 너무 부드럽거나 느리다.** 스피킹 답변은 사람 또는 컴퓨터에 의해 등급이 매겨진다. 목소리가 너무 부드럽거나 느려서 컴퓨터가 알아듣지 못하면 내용이 완벽해도 낮은 점수를 받는다.

단계별 답변 방법

1) 대학 공고문이나 학생의 편지를 45초간 읽는다. 리딩이 다시 나타나지 않으므로 메모하라.

2) 두 학생의 대화를 들어라. 대화는 한 번만 들려주므로 체계적으로 메모를 기록하라.

3) 30초 안에 답변을 준비한다. 이 시간 동안, 당신은 적은 메모를 연결하거나 대답을 연습할 수 있다.

4) 60초 안에 응답하라.

노트 테이킹:

정리된 필기를 하는 것이 중요하므로 스피킹 섹션을 시작하기 전에 필기를 준비하는 것이 좋다. 이 질문 유형에 대한 메모는 다음과 같은 방식으로 정리되어야 한다.

Announcement/Student letter main idea:

Detail 1:

Detail 2 :

Man	Woman
Opinion:	Opinion:
Reason 1:	Reason 1:
Details:	Details:
Reason 2:	Reason 2:
Details:	Details:

Page.43

리딩 섹션:

수험생들이 이 문제에서 낮은 점수를 받는 데는 여러 가지 이유가 있다.

주어진 45초 동안 리딩 지문이 공고인지 학생의 편지인지 먼저 확인해야 한다. 쉽게 구분할 수 있는 방법은 다음과 같다:

1) 대학 공고문은 상위에 타이틀을 달게 된다.

2) 학생의 편지는 누구에게 또는 그룹에게 보내는 주소부터 시작해서 누구로부터 온 것인지로 마무리한다. 가끔 '나는' 이나 '우리' 같은 1인칭 대명사가 쓰일 때가 있다.

수험생들이 다음으로 해야 할 일은 리딩 지문의 주요 아이디어를 찾는 것이다.

1) 대학 공고문의 주요 아이디어는 제목에 간결하게 기술되어 있다. 보다 정교한 주 아이디어는 그 구절의 첫 번째 문장이나 두 번째 문장에서 찾을 수 있다.

2) 학생의 편지의 주요 아이디어는 편지의 첫 번째 문장이나 두 번째 문장에서 찾을 수 있다.

마지막으로, 45초에서 남은 시간이 있다면, 리딩의 탄탄한 요약을 제공하기 위해 한두 개의 사소한 세부 사항을 쓰도록 하라. 세부적인 것은 대개 중심 생각의 이유나 효과다.

예시:

캠퍼스 투어 가이드

오랫동안 캠퍼스 투어 가이드는 대학 진학을 희망하는 예비 학생들을 위해 교수진이 주도해 왔다. 하지만 다음 학기부터는 대학생들이 직접 투어를 주도하게 된다. 교직원들은 더 이상 캠퍼스 투어를 이끌 시간이 없다. 그들은 다른 중요한 문제들에 자원을 집중해야 하며, 따라서 캠퍼스 투어를 할 인력이 없다. 게다가, 대학은 대학생들이 교수들이 갖지 못한 귀중한 통찰력을 제공할 수 있을 것으로 믿고 있다.

리스닝 섹션:

대화는 1분이 조금 넘는다. 발표나 편지에 대해 토론하는 두 학생의 대화를 들어야 할 것이다. 당신은 학생들이 말하는 모든 것을 적어야 한다. 이 문제에서 만점을 받기 위해서는 대화에서 언급된 작은 세부 사항까지 포함시켜야 하기 때문에 사소한 세부 사항을 쓰는 것이 중요하다.

이제 두 학생이 그 기사에 대해 토론하는 것을 들으시오.

M: 그래, 그 문제에 대해 어떻게 생각해?
W: 난 그게 좋다고 생각해. 오래 전에 일어났어야 할 일이야.
M: 왜 그렇게 생각해?
W: 난 최근에 수업 정보를 얻기 위해 학과 사무실에 갔었는데, 사무실에 있는 모든 사람들이 너무 바빴어. 그런 장면을 본 건 처음이 아니었어. 행정적인 질문을 하러 사무실에 갈 때마다 교직원들은 전화를 받거나 길게 줄 서 있는 학생들을 돕거나 쌓여 있는 서류 뒤에서 일하느라 바빴어. 교직원들이 투어를 이끌지 않는 것이 그들에게 휴식이 될 것 같아.
M: 난 그들이 그렇게 바쁜지 몰랐어.
W: 또한, 대학생들이 제시하는 가치 있는 통찰력에 대한 부분이야.
W: 난 대학생들이 정말 귀중한 정보를 제공할 수 있다고 생각해.
입학 예정자들과 나눌 수 있는 많은 경험이 있다는 것을 알고 있어. 학교 오기 전에 캠퍼스 투어에 참석했던 기억이 나. 투어를 이끄는 교수진도 좋았지만, 그들은 학생들이 던진 질문 중 일부에 대해서는 답을 하지 못했어.
M: 어떤 거?
W: 실제적인 것들이야. 어느 카페테리아가 가장 맛있는 음식을 제공하는지. 어느 기숙사가 가장 조용한지. 어느 도서관이 공부 환경이 제일 좋은지. 이런 것들 말이야. 교수진이 직접 경험하지 못한 것에 대한 질문들 말이야.
M: 그렇구나. 우리의 관점이 더 도움이 될 것 같아.

Page.48

문제

여자는 대학의 계획에 대해 자신의 의견을 말한다. 계획을 간략히 요약하라. 그리고 나서 그 계획에 대한 그녀의 의견을 진술하고 그녀가 그 의견을 지지하는 이유를 설명하라.

예시 답안

대학 공고문에 따르면 재학생들이 예비 학생들을 위한 캠퍼스 투어를 이끌 것이라고 한다. 이전에는 교수진이 했지만 더 이상 투어를 이끌 시간이 없다. 재학생들은 방문객들에게 독특하고 가치 있는 통찰력을 제공할 것이다.

대화에서 여자는 다음과 같은 이유로 공고문에 동의한다. 우선, 그녀는 전에 교무실에 가본 적이 있고, 그녀가 거기에 갈 때마다 그들은 매우 바빴다. 직원들은 전화를 받고, 긴 줄을 서서 학생들을 돕고, 서류 작업에도 주의를 기울이느라 바쁘다. 이 여성은 교직원들이 이 투어를 이끌지 않는 것이 그들에게 휴식을 줄 것이라고 믿고 있다.

게다가, 그녀는 대학생들이 귀중한 통찰력을 제공할 수 있을 것이라고 믿는다. 그녀는 전해줄 많은 경험이 있다. 그녀가 오래 전에 투어에 참여 했을 때, 투어를 이끌었던 교수는 좋은 사람이었지만, 경험해 보지 않아 대답할 수 없는 질문들이 있었다. 어느 카페테리아에 좋은 음식이 있는지, 어떤 기숙사가 가장 조용한지, 어떤 도서관이 공부하기에 가장 좋은지 등과 같은 실용적인 질문들. 교수진들은 그런 질문에 대답할 수 있는 직접적인 경험이 없었다.

따라서 여성이 공고에 동의하는 이유는 다음과 같다.

30초동안 답변을 준비할 수 있다는 것을 기억하라. 이 시간을 현명하게 사용하라. 아이디어를 연결하거나 메모한 정보의 요약을 순서대로 구성할 수 있다. 아니면 큰 소리로 말하면서 당신의 답변을 연습하기 시작하라. 머릿속에서 답변을 검토하는 것은 말로 하는 답변과 다르다. 30초로는 전체 답변을 완료하는 데 충분하지 않지만, 적어도 전체 답변을 하기 전에 절반의 시간 동안 연습할 수 있다.

연습1

Question 2 of 4
국제 뉴스 지난 몇 년간 대학 캠퍼스 신문에는 전 세계 주요 기사 몇 편을 취재한 국제 뉴스가 1페이지짜리 칼럼으로 실렸다. 그러나 이 섹션은 다음 달부터 없어진다. 이러한 변화의 이유 중 하나는 다른 뉴스 자료가 캠퍼스 신문보다 더 상세한 정보와 최신 뉴스를 더 잘 제공할 수 있기 때문이다. 게다가, 국제 뉴스 코너가 삭제된 곳에는 캠퍼스에서 일어나는 사건들과 활동들을 적은 새로운 달력 페이지로 채워질 것이다. 여자는 국제 뉴스 코너를 없애려는 계획에 대한 자신의 의견을 밝힌다. 그녀의 의견과 그녀가 그 의견을 주장하는 이유를 설명하시오.

M: So what do you think about the change?

W: Are you talking about the university newspaper's decision?

M: Uh huh.

W: I think it's a great idea. It's the right thing to do.

M: Really? How come?

W: Well, hardly anyone reads that section. I mean none of my friends read it.

M: Is that so?

W: The international news section only covers a few stories, and most of the people already heard the news before reading the campus newspaper.

M: I guess you're right. If you read the local newspapers or look at the internet, you already know what's going on.

W: Exactly. And there is much more information as well. I think the newspaper should just stick with campus news.

M: So do you think replacing the section with a calendar is better?

W: Of course. Right now, how do you know what's going on around campus?

M: Well I look at the posters on the different buildings, or the student center.

W: Exactly. The information is everywhere! So it's hard to keep track of it. I forget half of the announcements I see on the posters. With the new calendar section, I can just cut out the calendar, check it out anytime, and not lose track of what's going on around campus.

M: Seems like a good idea!

M: 그럼 그 변화에 대해 어떻게 생각해?

W: 대학 신문의 결정에 대해 말하는 거야?

M: 응.

W: 좋은 생각인 것 같아. 그것은 잘한 일이야.

M: 그래? 왜?

W: 글쎄, 그 부분을 읽는 사람은 거의 없어. 내 말은, 내 친구들 중 아무도 그것을 읽지 않는다는 거야.

M: 그래?

W: 국제 뉴스 섹션은 몇 가지 이야기만 다루고, 대부분의 사람들은 캠퍼스 신문을 읽기 전에 이미 그 소식을 듣지.

M: 네 말이 맞는 것 같아. 지역 신문을 읽거나 인터넷을 보면 이미 무슨 일이 벌어지고 있는지 알 수 있어.

W: 맞아. 그리고 훨씬 더 많은 정보도 있어. 나는 신문이 캠퍼스 뉴스만 실어야 한다고 생각해.

M: 그럼 너는 달력으로 그 부분을 대체하는 게 더 낫다고 생각해?

W: 물론이지. 너는 지금 캠퍼스 주위에서 무슨 일이 일어나고 있는지 어떻게 알아?

M: 글쎄, 난 다른 건물이나 학생 센터에 있는 포스터를 봐.

W: 맞아. 정보는 어디에나 있어! 그래서 그것을 계속 기억하기가 어려워. 나는 이미 포스터에서 본 공지 사항의 반을 까먹었어. 새로운 달력 섹션으로 달력을 오려 놓으면, 언제든 체크할 수 있고, 캠퍼스 주위에서 무슨 일이 일어나고 있는지 놓치지 않을 거야.

M: 좋은 생각 같아!

예시 답안

대학 측은 다음 달부터 국제 뉴스 코너가 일간 캠퍼스 신문에서 삭제된다고 밝히고 있다. 이러한 변화의 이유는 다른 뉴스 자료가 더 넓고 더 최신의 국제 뉴스를 제공할 수 있기 때문이다. 또한, 삭제된 공간에는 캠퍼스 주변의 이벤트와 활동을 나열하는 새로운 달력 페이지를 만들 것이다.

대화에서 여자는 다음과 같은 이유로 대학 측 발표에 동의한다.

우선, 그녀는 국제 뉴스 섹션을 거의 아무도 읽지 않는다고 말한다. 이 섹션은 아주 적은 뉴스만을 보여주며 대부분의 학생들은 그 뉴스가 종이에 인쇄되기 전에 이미 알고 있다. 그녀는 외부 소식통의 보도가 더 낫다고 믿는다. 그녀는 뉴스레터가 캠퍼스 뉴스에만 초점을 맞춰야 한다고 조언한다.

게다가, 그녀는 캠퍼스 행사와 뉴스가 어디에나 게시되어 있어서 그것을 기억하기가 힘들다고 말한다. 그녀는 공지가 올라오는 것을 보지만, 절반은 잊어버린다. 그녀는 신문에서 이 새로운 섹션을 잘라내고, 가지고 다닐 수 있으며, 언제 어디서 무슨 일이 일어나고 있는지 확인할 수 있다.

따라서, 이러한 이유들이 이 여자가 대학 측 발표에 동의하는 이유다.

연습2

<table>
<tr><td colspan="2" align="center">Question 2 of 4</td></tr>
<tr><td colspan="2" align="center">캠퍼스 커피 하우스 폐쇄</td></tr>
<tr><td colspan="2">저는 캠퍼스 커피 하우스를 대학이 폐쇄해야 한다고 생각합니다. 오해하지 마세요. 커피숍은 커피 한 잔 마시면서 친구들을 만나기에 좋은 곳이죠. 하지만 아무도 캠퍼스 커피 하우스를 이용하지 않아요. 커피숍 옆을 지날 때마다 빈 좌석과 테이블이 보입니다. 커피 하우스는 더 유용한 것을 위해 사용될 수 있는 공간을 낭비하고 있습니다. 게다가, 그곳에서 제공되는 음식들은 맛있지 않아요. 지난번에 친구랑 갔을 때 우리가 주문한 머핀과 케이크는 건조하고, 맛이 없었습니다. - 토마스 존슨 올림</td></tr>
<tr><td colspan="2">여자는 편집자에게 보낸 학생의 편지에 대한 자신의 의견을 말한다. 그녀의 의견과 그 의견을 주장하는 이유를 설명하시오</td></tr>
<tr>
<td>

Now listen to two students discussing the letter.
W: I don't agree with what Thomas said in his letter.
M: How come? I don't see a lot of students at the coffeehouse.
W: But that's what makes it appealing. It's never crowded, so it's a great place to study. I go there often to read a good book, or work on a paper with my laptop. It's not noisy so I can be productive in my work.
M: Can you actually study there?
W: Of course! I actually prefer the coffeehouse to the library when it comes to studying. Many of my friends think similarly, and we study for our finals there as well. We can also eat while we study, which is something we can't do at the library.
M: Ok, but do you really like the food that is served there?
W: Well, the food has actually improved in taste recently. It is true that the food was not so tasty in the past, but it's a lot better now.
M: Oh? How come?
W: Well, they hired a new manager and she made some improvements in the quality of the food served there. Just last week, I went to study there, and the food tasted great.
M: Really?
W: Yup. And the new manager added healthy alternatives as well. So the food not only tastes great, but it's healthy for you.
M: I will definitely check the coffeehouse sometime this week.

</td>
<td>

두 학생이 편지에 대해 이야기 하는 것을 들으시오.
W: 난 토마스가 편지에서 한 말에 동의하지 않아.
M: 왜? 나는 커피숍에 많은 학생들이 있는 걸 못 봤어.
W: 오히려 그게 매력적인 이유야. 전혀 붐비지 않아서 공부하기 좋은 곳이지. 나는 종종 좋은 책을 읽거나, 노트북으로 과제를 하기 위해 그곳에 가. 시끄럽지 않아서 일을 할 때 생산적일 수 있어.
M: 정말 거기서 공부할 수 있어?
W: 물론이지! 사실 나는 공부하는 데 있어서 도서관보다 커피하우스가 더 좋아. 내 많은 친구들도 비슷한 생각을 하고 있어서 우리는 기말고사 공부도 거기서 하고 있어. 공부하면서 식사도 할 수 있는데, 도서관에서는 할 수 없는 일이야.
M: 그래, 근데 거기 나오는 음식들을 정말 좋아하니?
W: 음, 최근에 음식이 실제로 맛이 좋아졌어. 예전에는 음식이 그렇게 맛있지 않았던 것은 사실이지만 지금은 많이 좋아졌어.
M: 어? 어떻게 된 거지?
W: 음, 그들은 새로운 매니저를 고용했고, 그 매니저는 음식의 질을 향상시켰어. 바로 지난주에, 나는 그곳에 공부하러 갔었는데, 음식 맛이 아주 좋았어.
M: 그래?
W: 응. 그리고 그 새로운 매니저는 건강식도 추가했어. 그래서 그 음식은 맛이 좋을 뿐만 아니라 건강에도 좋아.
M: 이번 주 중에 커피하우스에 꼭 들러 볼게.

</td>
</tr>
</table>

예시 답변

학생의 편지에는 캠퍼스 커피하우스를 폐쇄해야 한다는 내용이 적혀 있다. 학생들이 커피숍을 이용하지 않고 그가 지나갈 때마다 빈 테이블이 많기 때문이다. 또한, 그곳의 음식은 그렇게 썩 맛있지 않다.

대화에서 여자는 다음과 같은 이유로 그 편지에 동의하지 않는다.

우선 그녀는 커피 하우스가 전혀 붐비지 않아서 공부하기 좋은 장소이기 때문에 그곳을 좋아한다. 그녀는 그곳이 시끄럽지 않기 때문에 수업 시간에 책을 읽거나 과제를 하기 위해 그곳에 자주 간다. 그녀와 다른 학생들은 기말고사를 위해 공부하는 장소로 도서관보다 커피 하우스를 선호한다. 왜냐하면 그들이 공부를 하면서 식사도 할 수 있기 때문이다.

게다가, 그녀는 필자가 최근에 커피숍에 간 적이 없다고 믿는다. 그녀는 과거에는 음식이 좋지 않았다는 것을 인정하지만, 커피숍에 새로운 매니저가 왔고, 음식의 질이 좋아졌기 때문에 지금은 더 나아졌다. 그 여자는 지난주에 그곳에 갔었고, 음식이 맛있다고 말했다. 또한 새로운 매니저가 건강한 음식과 간식을 추가했고, 그것은 맛도 좋고 몸에도 좋다.

따라서 이것들이 그 여자가 학생의 편지에 동의하지 않는 이유들이다.

연습3

<table>
<tr><td colspan="2" align="center">Question 2 of 1</td></tr>
<tr><td colspan="2" align="center">별도 졸업</td></tr>
<tr><td colspan="2">대학에서는 애초에 졸업생 전원을 대상으로 졸업장을 수여하는 한 번의 졸업식만을 열고 있다. 하지만 올해부터 이 대학은 두 번의 별도의 졸업식을 갖는다. 첫날에는 졸업반 절반 이상이 참석하고, 다음날에는 나머지 절반이 참석한다. 이러한 변화에는 두 가지 이유가 있다. 첫째, 입학생이 증가하고 학생 한 명 한 명에게 졸업장을 나눠 주면서 식이 너무 길어졌다. 더욱이 이들이 졸업식을 치르는 식장은 관객들을 수용하기에는 규모가 너무 작다.</td></tr>
<tr><td colspan="2">여자는 대학의 계획에 대한 자신의 의견을 표명한다. 그녀의 의견과 그녀가 그 의견을 주장하는 이유를 설명하시오.</td></tr>
<tr><td>

Now listen to a conversation between two students regarding the announcement.

W: I can't believe the university is doing this!

M: Why?

W: I think it's completely unnecessary. First, yes, it does take a long time for the students to get the diplomas individually since there are more students than before. However, there is a way to make the ceremony shorter.

M: Which is?

W: By minimizing the number of speeches that are given at the ceremony. Right now, so many people give their speeches at the graduation ceremony. Students, professors, administrators, the president of the university…. I don't think we need to hear that many speeches.

M: I agree. A lot of the speeches are boring too. So I think people would not mind if we shorten the number of speeches.

W: Yup. Also, I disagree with the second reason, about the space in the ceremony hall.

M: How so?

W: The main problem does not lie with the size of the hall, rather, students invite too many people to the ceremony. If the university reduces the number of guests each student can invite, that would solve the problem.

M: I guess that would work.

W: It will work! Right now, students are allowed to invite up to 10 people to the ceremony which is a lot. Other schools limit their graduating students to invite only 4 or 5 people. If the university limits the number of people students can invite to 6, that would still be more than other schools and the ceremony will not have to be held in two different days.

</td><td>

두 학생이 발표문에 대해 이야기 하는 내용을 들으시오.

W: 대학이 이런 짓을 하다니 믿을 수가 없어!

M: 왜?

W: 난 그게 전혀 불필요하다고 생각해. 첫째로, 물론 학생들이 이전보다 많아졌기 때문에 학생들이 개별적으로 졸업장을 받기까지 오랜 시간이 걸려. 하지만 식을 짧게 하는 방법이 있어.

M: 그게 뭔데?

W: 시상식에서 연설하는 횟수를 최소화하는 거야. 지금, 너무나 많은 사람들이 졸업식에서 연설을 해. 학생, 교수, 행정관, 대학 총장 등등. 나는 우리가 그렇게 많은 연설을 들을 필요가 없다고 생각해.

M: 동의해. 또한 많은 연설들이 지루해. 그래서 나는 우리가 연설 횟수를 줄여도 사람들이 신경 쓰지 않을 거라고 생각해.

W: 응. 그리고, 나는 식장의 공간과 관련된 두 번째 이유에도 동의할 수 없어.

M: 왜?

W: 주된 문제는 식장의 크기에 있는 것이 아니라, 학생들이 너무 많은 사람들을 식에 초대하는 거야. 대학이 학생 한 명 한 명이 초대할 수 있는 손님 수를 줄이면 문제가 해결될 거야.

M: 그게 효과가 있을 것 같아.

W: 그럴 거야! 지금은 학생들이 식에 10명까지 초대할 수 있는데, 너무 많아. 다른 학교에서는 졸업생이 4, 5명만 초대하도록 제한하고 있어. 대학이 학생들을 초대할 수 있는 인원을 6명으로 제한한다면, 이는 여전히 다른 학교들보다 많을 것이지만, 식이 이틀 간 열릴 필요는 없을 거야.

</td></tr>
</table>

예시 답변

대학 측은 올해부터 두 차례 졸업식을 개최한다고 밝혔다. 이 같은 변화의 이유는 최근 몇 년간 학생 수가 증가해 식이 너무 길었기 때문이다. 또한, 식장이 너무 작아서 가족, 친구들과 함께 많은 수의 학생들을 수용할 수 없을 것이기 때문이다.

대화에서 여자는 다음과 같은 이유로 대학 측 발표에 동의하지 않는다.

우선, 그녀는 그것이 불필요하다고 믿는다. 그녀는 학생들이 개별적으로 졸업장을 받기까지 오랜 시간이 걸릴 것이라는 데에는 동의하지만, 시간을 줄이는 더 쉬운 방법은 연설 횟수를 줄이는 것이라고 믿는다. 학생, 교수, 행정가, 총장이 모두 연설을 하는데, 그녀는 이것들이 불필요하다고 생각한다.

게다가, 그녀는 식장의 크기가 문제가 아니라 학생들이 너무 많은 사람들을 초대하는 것이 문제라고 믿는다. 학교는 학생들이 초대할 수 있는 손님 수를 줄여야 한다. 현재 졸업생들은 10명을 초대할 수 있는데, 이는 다른 학교에서 4~5명을 초대하는 것에 비해 너무 많은 것이다. 여자는 6명을 초대하는 것이 적당하며, 그렇게 식이 진행될 수 있다고 믿는다.

따라서 이것들이 여자가 대학 측 발표에 동의하지 않는 이유들이다.

연습4

Question 2 of 4

지도 교수와의 불필요한 만남

현재 이 대학은 매 학기 시작 전에 학생들이 지도 교수와 만나는 것을 의무화했다. 지도 교수는 학생들이 어떤 과정을 수강할 것인지 선택하는 것뿐만 아니라 졸업 요건에 대해서도 도움을 준다. 유감스럽게도, 나는 이 만남의 요점을 모르겠다. 왜냐하면 그 강좌에 대한 정보는 이미 대학 웹 사이트에 게시되어 있기 때문이다. 또한, 지도 교수와 만날 필요가 없다면, 학생들은 자신과 지도 교수가 모두 한가할 때 회의 일정을 잡는 번거로움을 겪지 않아도 될 것이다. - 사라 존슨 올림

남자는 편지 속 제안에 대한 자신의 의견을 표현한다. 제안을 요약한 다음, 남자의 의견을 진술하고 그 의견의 근거를 설명하시오.

Now listen to two students discussing the letter:
M: Did you see the letter Sarah wrote?
W: Sure did. What's up?
M: I don't agree with her. It's not the same information that is uploaded on the university website.
W: Are you sure? It seems pretty similar to me.
M: I mean sure, the basic information on the internet is the same information that advisors provide. But advisors give more than that. In certain circumstances, there are different ways to meet the graduation requirements, such as different courses you can take. By talking with academic advisors, they can help you figure that out.
W: Ah, so you can't get that kind of information from the website.
M: Yes. Advisors have lots of useful information that cannot be found on the website, and they make it easier to see what choices you have.
W: Uh huh, I see.
M: Also, the part about scheduling a meeting with the advisor… I never had problems making an appointment with an advisor.
W: Me too.
M: So if anyone has a problem with making an appointment with the advisor, they are waiting to make the appointment till the last minute.
W: That is possible.
M: If you call or go to the academic office to make an appointment ahead of time, there are lots of time slots open to make an appointment with the advisor. Waiting until the last day to make the appointment will be harder because all of the other slots will have been taken.
W: I see what you mean.

이제 두 학생이 편지에 대해 토론하는 것을 들으시오.
M: 사라가 쓴 편지 봤어?
W: 당연하지. 무슨 일이야?
M: 난 그녀에게 동의하지 않아. 대학 홈페이지에 올라오는 것과 같은 정보가 아니야.
W: 확실해? 나는 꽤 비슷한 것 같아.
M: 내 말은, 인터넷의 기본 정보는 지도 교수들이 제공하는 것과 같은 정보야. 하지만 지도 교수들은 그것보다 많은 것을 줘. 어떤 상황에서는 수강할 수 있는 강좌가 달라지는 등 졸업 요건을 충족시키는 방법이 달라. 지도 교수와 대화함으로써 그것들을 알아내는 데 도움을 받을 수 있어.
W: 아, 그러니까 웹사이트에서 그런 종류의 정보는 얻을 수 없다는 거지.
M: 응. 지도 교수들은 웹사이트에서 찾을 수 없는 많은 유용한 정보를 가지고 있고, 우리에게 어떤 선택지가 있는지 더 쉽게 볼 수 있게 해 줘.
W: 음, 그렇구나.
M: 또한, 지도 교수와 만남 일정을 정하는 부분… 나는 지도 교수와 약속을 잡는 데 전혀 문제가 없었어.
W: 나도 그래.
M: 그래서, 지도 교수와 약속을 하는 데 문제가 있는 사람이 있다면, 그들은 마지막 순간까지 약속을 잡으려고 기다리겠지.
W: 그건 가능해.
M: 미리 전화하거나 학과 사무실에 가서 약속을 잡으면, 지도 교수와 약속을 잡을 수 있는 시간이 많이 열려 있어. 마지막 날까지 기다린다면 모든 다른 일정이 잡혀서 약속 잡기가 더 힘들 거야.
W: 무슨 말인지 알겠어.

예시 답변

그 학생의 편지에는 그녀가 지도 교수와의 만남의 요점을 찾지 못하겠다고 쓰여 있다. 강좌에 대한 정보는 이미 대학 홈페이지에서 확인할 수 있으며, 모두가 다 여유로울 때 지도 교수와 만날 시간을 잡기가 어려운 점도 있다.

대화에서 남자는 다음과 같은 이유로 편지에 동의하지 않는다. 우선, 그는 웹 사이트에서 발견되는 정보가 똑같은 것이 아니라고 말한다. 기본적인 정보는 거기에 있지만, 지도교수들은 그것보다 더 많은 것을 제공한다. 졸업요건은 마치 수업들이 다른 것처럼 다르다. 누군가와 대화함으로써, 그 사람은 그것을 알아내는데 도움을 받을 수 있다. 지도교수들은 많은 추가 정보를 가지고 있기 때문에 그들은 선택지들이 무엇인지 더 쉽게 알 수 있다.

게다가, 그 남자는 만남 일정을 잡는데 전혀 어려움을 겪지 않았다. 일정을 잡는 데 문제가 있는 사람은 만남을 위해 마지막 순간까지 기다리고 있다. 학생들이 일찍 전화를 걸거나 사무실로 일찍 찾아가면, 만남을 가질 수 있다. 마지막 순간까지 기다리면 지도 교수와 만나는 것이 더 어려워진다.

그러므로, 이러한 이유들이 그 남자가 학생의 편지에 동의하지 않는 이유이다.

연습5

<table>
<tr><td colspan="2" align="center">Question 2 of 4</td></tr>
<tr><td colspan="2" align="center">전자 교과서</td></tr>
<tr><td colspan="2">이 대학은 내년 초부터 전통적인 교과서에서 전자 교과서로 전환할 예정이다. 학생들은 자신의 기기를 사용하여 교과서를 다운로드 받고 기기에서 직접 자료를 읽을 수 있게 된다. 전자 기기의 비용은 약 200달러지만, 이것은 일회성 결제가 될 것이다. 교과서의 최근 몇 년 동안의 비용 증가를 고려할 때 학생들은 돈을 절약할 수 있을 것이다. 수업용 전자 교과서는 일반 교과서를 사는 것보다 훨씬 더 저렴할 것이다. 또 전자 교과서는 조작이 용이하고 텍스트 강조, 노트 필기 등의 특징이 있어 훌륭한 학습 도구가 될 것으로 학교 측은 보고 있다.</td></tr>
<tr><td colspan="2">여자는 대학의 계획에 대해 자신의 의견을 표현한다. 계획을 간단히 요약한 후 그녀의 의견을 진술하고 그녀가 그 의견을 제시한 근거를 설명하시오.</td></tr>
<tr>
<td>

Listen to two students discussing the announcement.
W: Oh no, did you see the announcement?
M: Sure did. Why, you don't like electronic textbooks?
W: Sure don't. First, there's the cost. The school is not being realistic in the devices' cost.
M: Are you saying that the device's cost is still expensive even after being compared to the cost of a traditional textbook?
W: Of course, textbooks are not cheap. But do you really think that students will use just one device the entire time they are enrolled in the university? If the device breaks, you would have to buy a new one. Or if the device comes out with new features, you would want to replace your old one as well.
M: I guess a lot of people would want to get the latest device when it comes out.
W: Exactly. And new devices come out every year, which can add up in costs.
M: I guess you're right. But don't you agree that the electronic textbook will help studying to be easier with its great features?
W: I'm not sure if a lot of the students will think it will be easier.
M: How come?
W: It would be easy to use, but the device is pretty small. It's only 18 to 20 centimeters tall.
M: Oh wow, that means the screen is pretty small.
W: Yup. Even the keypad and control buttons are small as well. So with normal sized fingers, it will be difficult to select items or use the features on the device, like highlighting or underlining.
M: That didn't cross my mind.
W: So what good are the features if the user is unable to use them comfortably? I actually like the traditional way of studying. I like to write my notes on the page, underlining and highlighting the important points in the book. I'm just more comfortable with that.

</td>
<td>

두 학생이 발표에 대해 토론하는 것을 들으시오.
W: 어떡해, 안내 방송 봤어?
M: 당연하지. 왜, 너는 전자 교과서를 싫어해?
W: 물론 안 좋아하지. 첫째로, 비용이 들어. 학교는 기기 비용에 현실적이지 않아.
M: 심지어 전통적인 교과서의 가격과 비교해도?
W: 물론, 교과서는 싸지 않아. 하지만 정말 학생들이 대학에 등록하는 내내 하나의 기기만 사용할 것이라고 생각해? 기기가 고장 나면 새 것을 사야 할 거야. 또는 기기에 새로운 기능이 추가되면 이전 기기를 교체하고 싶을 거야.
M: 아마 많은 사람들이 최신 기기가 나오면 그걸 갖고 싶어할 거야.
W: 맞아. 그리고 매년 새로운 기기들이 출시되고, 이것은 비용을 증가시킬 수 있어.
M: 네 말이 맞는 것 같아. 하지만 너는 전자 교과서가 지닌 훌륭한 기능이 공부를 더 쉽게 하는데 도움이 될 것이라 생각하지 않아?
W: 난 많은 학생들이 왜 그게 더 쉬울 거라고 생각할지는 잘 모르겠어.
M: 왜?
W: 사용하기 편하겠지만, 그 장치는 꽤 작잖아. 높이가 18~20cm밖에 안 돼.
M: 와, 그건 화면이 꽤 작다는 뜻이네.
W: 응. 키패드나 제어 버튼도 작잖아. 따라서 정상적인 크기의 손가락으로는 강조 표시나 밑줄 긋기와 같이 기기에서 항목을 선택하거나 기능을 사용하는 것이 어려울 거야.
M: 그건 생각 못했어.
W: 사용자가 기능들을 편안하게 사용할 수 없다면 어떤 점이 좋은 걸까? 나는 사실 전통적인 공부 방식을 좋아해. 나는 책에 있는 중요한 사항들에 밑줄을 긋고 강조하면서 페이지에 메모 하는 것을 좋아해. 난 그게 더 편해.

</td>
</tr>
</table>

예시 답변

이 대학 발표에 따르면 이 학교는 내년 초에 전통적인 교과서에서 전자 교과서로 전환될 것이라고 한다. 학생들은 전자 기기를 위한 일회성 비용만 지불하면 될 것이다. 이 장치는 조작이 간단하고 효과적인 학습 보조 장치가 되도록 많은 기능을 제공한다.

대화에서 여자는 다음과 같은 이유로 발표에 동의하지 않는다.

우선, 그녀는 그 비용이 현실적이지 않다고 말한다. 그녀는 교과서가 비싸다는 것을 인정하지만, 학생들이 항상 하나의 기기를 사용하는 것은 아니라고 생각한다. 기기가 고장 나면 학생들은 다른 기기를 구입해야 하며, 기기가 뛰어난 기능으로 업그레이드되면 학생들은 업그레이드를 원할 것이다. 학생들이 매년 기기를 교체하면 비용이 추가될 것이다. 게다가, 모든 사람이 이 장치의 혜택을 받는 것은 아니다. 학생들이 그것을 어떻게 사용하는지 알아야만 도움이 될 것이다. 이 장치는 높이가 18~20cm에 불과할 정도로 작다. 키패드와 컨트롤 버튼도 작다. 그래서 보통 크기의 손가락을 가진 사람들은 항목을 선택하거나 그것을 제대로 작동시키는 데 어려움을 겪을 것이다. 따라서 사용자가 사용하지 못한다면 화려한 기능이 좋을 것은 없다. 여자는 페이지에 메모를 하고 책의 중요한 부분에 밑줄을 긋거나 강조하는 등의 옛날 방식을 선호한다.

그러므로, 이러한 이유들이 그 여성이 발표에 동의하지 않는 근거이다.

Chapter03
Q3 General to Specific

Q3. 일반적인 것에서 구체적인 것으로

이 문제 유형에서는 학술적인 리딩과 리딩 내용 관련 강의를 요약한다. 주요 아이디어를 얼마나 잘 요약할 수 있는지, 리딩과 리스닝에 언급된 내용을 바탕으로 포인트가 주어진다. 답변을 준비할 시간은 30초, 답변을 녹음할 시간은 60초가 주어진다.

문제는 어떻게 제시되는가:

> 교수는 자동차 공장에 대해 이야기한다. 4차 산업 혁명과 어떤 관련이 있는지 설명하라.
> 리딩에서는 4차 산업 혁명을, 강연에서는 자동차 공장에 대해 논의한다.

> 교수는 웨이터로 일한 경험을 말한다. 그것이 어떻게 협력과 관련이 있는지 설명하라.
> 리딩 지문은 협력에 대해 이야기하고, 강의는 웨이터로 일하는 교수에 대해 논의한다.

> 그 교수는 온라인 게임에 대해 말한다. 그것이 소셜 네트워크와 어떻게 관련이 있는지 설명하라.
> 리딩에서는 소셜 네트워크에 대해, 강의에서는 온라인 게임에 대해 논의한다

Answers and Script   32

Page.69~72

왜 이 문항에서 낮은 점수를 받는가?

수험생들이 이 문제에서 낮은 점수를 받는 데는 여러 이유가 있다.

1) **잘린 응답.** 60초에서 응답이 끊기는 불완전한 응답을 하는 것은 더 낮은 점수를 받는다는 것에 유의해야 한다. 단절된 응답보다 55초간 답변을 하고, 5초 가량 침묵하는 것이 좋다.

2) **세부 사항 부족.** 이 답변은 리딩과 리스닝을 얼마나 잘 요약할 수 있느냐에 기초한다. 리딩을 읽고 강의를 들을 때는 반드시 잘 메모하고, 답변에 그 세부 사항을 언급하라.

3) **언급되지 않았거나 잘못 표현된 정보.** 때때로 수험생들은 리딩과 리스닝에 언급되지 않은 정보를 포함하게 된다. 그들은 이 문제에 관한 배경 지식 혹은 개인적인 경험을 가지고 있거나, 정보를 잘못 들었을 수도 있기 때문에 이렇게 하는 경향이 있다. 리딩 및 리스닝에 언급된 정보만 포함하라. 또한, 정보가 잘못 주어질 수 있다. 언급된 내용을 이해하도록 최선을 다해라.

4) **조직되지 않은 답변.** 리딩의 요약이 먼저 제시되고, 그 다음에 리스닝이 나와야 한다. 이 질문 유형의 말하기 템플릿을 따르라.

5) **문법 오용.** 놀랍게도, 문법은 점수를 감점시키는 가장 큰 측면은 아니다. 기억하라, 토플 시험을 보는 대부분의 학생들은 원어민이 아닌 영어 사용자들이기 때문에 그들의 문법은 완벽하지 않을 것이다. 그래도 문법 실수가 너무 많으면 점수가 낮아진다.

6) **말이 너무 부드럽거나 느리다.** 당신의 스피킹 답변은 사람 또는 컴퓨터에 의해 등급이 매겨진다. 목소리가 너무 부드럽거나 느려서 컴퓨터가 알아듣지 못하면 내용이 완벽해도 낮은 점수를 받는다.

단계별 답변 방법:

1) 학술 지문을 50초간 읽는다. 리딩이 다시 나타나지 않으므로 메모하라.
2) 강의를 들어라. 강의는 한 번만 진행되므로 체계적으로 노트를 작성하라.
3) 30초 안에 반응을 준비한다. 이 시간 동안, 여러분은 여러분이 적은 노트를 정리하거나, 여러분의 답변을 연습을 할 수 있다.
4) 60초 안에 응답하라.

노트 테이킹:

정리된 필기를 하는 것이 중요하므로 스피킹 섹션을 시작하기 전에 필기를 준비하는 것이 좋다. 이 질문 유형에 대한 메모는 다음과 같은 방식으로 정리되어야 한다.

Title of the reading passage:
Definition or description of the title:
Detail:

Lecture's point 1:
Detail:
Lecture's point 2:
Detail:

리딩 섹션:

리딩에서는 강의의 전반적인 아이디어를 논할 것이다. 강의가 진행되기 전의 배경 지식이라고 생각하라. 리딩 구절이 나오면 먼저 리딩의 제목을 적는다. 제목은 강의뿐 아니라 리딩 구절의 주요 아이디어다. 그런 다음, 리딩 구절에서 제목의 정의나 설명을 빨리 찾아라.
정의나 서술의 가장 일반적인 방법: "(TITLE은) …"
남은 50초 동안, 리딩에서 뒷받침되는 세부 사항을 적어 보라.

예시

비합리적인 헌신

개인이 프로젝트에 많은 시간을 할애할 때, 그들은 긍정적인 결과를 보고 싶어 한다. 그러나 그들은 긍정적인 결과를 내는 것에 너무 집착한 나머지 비록 그 과정에서 실패한 결과물이 나타나기 시작하더라도, 이 사실을 무시한 채 좋은 결과를 내기 위해 더 열심히 노력할 것이다.
이것은 비합리적인 헌신으로 알려져 있다. 실제로 그만두는 것이 더 나음에도 프로젝트를 진행하려는 이러한 경향은, 자신의 성패가 다른 사람들에 의해 평가 받을 수 있다고 느낄 때 특히 강할 수 있다.

Page.73

리스닝 세션:

이 강의에서는 리딩에 관한 구체적인 예나 주제에 대해 논의한다. 대부분의 경우, 강의에서는 일반적인 주제에 관한 두 가지 주요 사항을 언급할 것이다. 그러나 때때로 교수는 일반적인 주제를 뒷받침하는 장시간의 개인적인 경험을 말할 수도 있다. 아무튼 메모를 꼼꼼히 하라.

강의는 2분 이내로 할 것이다. 가능한 한 많은 정보를 기록하려고 노력하는 것이 필수적이다. 여기에는 사물을 묘사하는 데 사용된 형용사뿐만 아니라 이름과 숫자도 포함된다. 요약하면 할수록 더 많은 포인트를 얻게 된다는 것을 기억하라.

심리학 수업의 일부를 들어라.

교수:
개인적인 예를 하나 들어봅시다. 몇 년 전, 아내와 나는 구매할 집을 찾고 있었습니다. 시골에서 우리가 좋아할 만한 물건을 찾았죠. 하지만 나의 아내는 그 집을 사는 데 주저했습니다. 그 집은 최상의 상태가 아니었고, 아마 약간의 수리가 필요할 것 같았죠. 하지만 나는 그 집이 정말 좋았는데, 특히 건축물과 특이한 건축 방식이 마음에 들었어요. 그래서 나는 아내에게 그 집을 수리할 사람들을 고용하자고 설득하였습니다. 우리는 그것이 수리된 후에 그 집에 살게 될 예정이었죠.

집을 수리하러 온 사람들은 곧 우리가 알지 못하는 다른 문제들을 발견했어요. 지붕이 파손되어 있어, 비용이 많이 드는 수리가 필요하단 것이었습니다. 일꾼들이 지붕 수리를 끝냈을 때, 그들은 집에 전기 문제가 있다는 것을 발견했어요. 대부분의 전선을 교체해야 했고, 이는 비용이 많이 들 것이 분명했죠. 아내는 집을 사기를 주저했다는 사실을 상기시켰지만, 나는 그 집을 내 것으로 만들고자 하는 마음이 더 강했어요. 나는 수리비를 지불했어요. 하지만 상황은 더 나빠졌죠.
벌레들이 벽의 일부를 먹어 버렸기 때문에 벽을 뜯어내고 교체해야 했어요. 사실 벽을 교체하는 것은 다른 모든 수리보다 비용이 더 많이 들겠지만, 이쯤 되니, 예상보다 더 큰 비용이 들더라도 집 수리를 끝내야겠다는 사명감이 들었어요. 만약 내가 포기하면, 아내가 자신의 충고를 따르지 않았다고 잔소리를 할 것 같다는 느낌이 들었죠!

예시 답변

리딩은 개인들이 긍정적인 결과를 내는 것에 너무 집착하게 되어, 비록 그 프로젝트가 실패할 것처럼 보이거나 단점이 이점을 뛰어넘는 데도 불구하고, 계속해서 프로젝트를 포기하지 않고 진행하려는 것으로 비합리적인 헌신의 개념을 논의한다. 이러한 비합리적인 헌신은 자신의 성패가 다른 사람들에 의해 평가될 수 있다고 느껴질 때, 특히 강할 수 있다.

이는 교수가 비합리적인 헌신을 설명하기 위해 사용하는 예다.

강의에서 교수는 개인적인 예를 든다. 몇 년 전 그와 그의 아내는 살 집을 찾고 있었다. 그들은 시골에 있는 오래된 집을 발견했지만, 그의 아내는 집의 상태가 좋지 않고 수리가 필요했기 때문에 내키지 않았다. 그러나 교수는 그 집의 건축 양식에 반했다. 그래서 교수는 집을 수리할 사람들을 고용하자고 아내를 설득하였다. 그들은 그 집을 사기로 결정했고, 수리가 끝난 후에 살기로 했다. 하지만, 일꾼들은 상황이 교수가 원래 생각했던 것보다 더 나쁘다는 것을 발견했다. 지붕이 파손되어 비싼 수리가 필요했다. 일꾼들은 전기 문제도 발견했다. 대부분의 전선을 교체해야 했는데, 비용이 많이 들 것이었다. 그때 교수의 아내는 그녀가 지녔던 의심을 그에게 상기시켰다. 그러나 그는 그 어느 때보다도 단호했고, 배선을 교체하기 위한 비용을 지불했다. 하지만, 설상가상으로 그들은 벌레들이 벽의 일부를 먹어 치웠다는 것을 발견했고, 벽을 뜯어내고 교체해야 했다. 이는 다른 모든 수리보다 더 비싼 것이었다. 그래도 교수는 이 일을 끝까지 해야 한다고 속으로 생각했고, 그렇지 않으면 아내가 그에게 충고를 따르지 않았다고 잔소리를 할 것이라고 생각했다.

다시 말하자면, 대부분의 경우 강의에는 리딩 지문의 일반적인 아이디어에 관한 두 가지 사항을 담고 있을 것이다. 그런 경우, 당신은 "To begin with"과 "Furthermore"라는 문구를 언급하면서 글의 초점을 나누어야 한다.

30초 동안 답변을 준비하는 것을 잊지 마라. 메모한 내용을 조직화하거나 더 잘 정리하거나, 큰 소리로 답변을 하는 연습을 해보길 권한다.

Page.77

연습1

Question 3 of 4

<table>
<tr><td colspan="2" align="center">준거 집단</td></tr>
<tr><td colspan="2">사람들은 우리가 생각하고 행동하는 방식에 영향을 미친다. 우리는 우리가 존경하고 칭찬하는 사람들의 행동과 태도를 모방하려는 경향이 있다. 우리가 존경하면서 행동과 태도를 따라 하고 싶어 하는 사람들을 준거 집단이라고 한다. 준거 집단은 우리가 생각하고 행동하는 방식에 영향을 줄 수 있는 준거 틀을 제공한다. 오랜 기간 동안, 우리는 다양한 준거 집단의 영향을 받을 수 있다. 우리가 나이를 먹거나 새로운 환경을 접하게 되면, 우리의 준거 집단이 바뀔 수도 있고, 그것은 우리의 태도와 행동을 새로운 방향으로 이끌 수도 있다.</td></tr>
<tr><td colspan="2">강의에 제시된 예를 들어, 사람들의 행동이 준거 집단에 의해 어떻게 영향을 받는지 설명하시오.</td></tr>
<tr>
<td>Now listen to a lecture on a sociology class on this topic.

Let me talk about a personal experience that illustrates this. When I entered the university as a freshmen, I became friends with some art students. They were older than me, fun, and creative. And I thought they were really cool. They all preferred to dress casually. They liked wearing jeans, t-shirts, and sneakers. They wore this everywhere they went: to class, library, and cafeteria. So I started to dress like them too. I was able to fit right in and I felt cool being in the group. Later I graduated, and got a job in Chicago. I worked alongside a bright group of individuals, who had already been working at the company for a few years. They were already taking care of major responsibilities, which I thought was very impressive. Sometimes, we would meet over the weekend to go watch a concert or a baseball game. I would wear my jeans, t-shirt, and sneakers since I was used to wearing the casual outfit. However, I noticed that my co-workers liked to dress up during these meetings. The guys would wear nice pants with a buttoned shirt, while the girls would wear a fashionable dress with some nice shoes. My co-workers would dress up in clothes that were a lot nicer than what I would wear. I started to think that the clothes they wore were very classy and sharp. And so I started to wear nicer clothes as well. The casual jeans, t-shirts, and sneakers no longer seemed cool to me.</td>
<td>이 주제에 관해 사회학 수업 시간에 이뤄지는 강의를 들으시오.

이것을 보여주는 개인적인 경험에 대해 이야기해 보겠습니다. 제가 신입생으로 대학에 들어갔을 때, 나는 몇몇 미대 학생들과 친구가 되었어요. 그들은 나보다 나이가 많고 재미있고 창의적이었죠. 그리고 나는 그들이 정말 멋지다고 생각해요. 그들은 모두 편안하게 입는 것을 선호했죠. 그들은 청바지, 티셔츠를 입고 운동화를 신는 것을 좋아했어요. 교실, 도서관, 카페테리아 등 가는 곳마다 그것을 입었죠. 그래서 저도 그들처럼 옷을 입기 시작했어요. 저는 그들과 잘 어울릴 수 있었고 그 그룹에 있는 것이 좋았어요. 나중에 저는 졸업해서, 시카고에서 일자리를 얻었어요. 저는 이미 몇 년 동안 회사에서 일해 온 전도유망한 팀 사람들과 함께 일했죠. 그들은 이미 주요한 책임을 맡고 있었는데, 그것은 매우 인상적이었습니다. 때때로, 우리는 주말에 만나서 콘서트나 야구 경기를 보러 가곤 했어요. 저는 편한 복장에 익숙했기 때문에 청바지, 티셔츠를 입고, 운동화를 신곤 했어요. 하지만, 저는 저의 동료들이 이런 모임에서 옷을 갖춰 입는 것을 좋아한다는 것을 알게 되었어요. 남자들은 단추가 달린 셔츠에 멋진 바지를 입고, 여자들은 멋진 신발과 함께 유행하는 드레스를 입곤 했죠. 제 동료들은 제가 입은 옷보다 훨씬 더 멋진 옷을 갖춰 입곤 했어요. 저는 그들이 입은 옷이 매우 품위 있고 멋지다고 생각하기 시작했어요. 그래서 저는 그들처럼 더 멋진 옷을 입기 시작했죠. 캐주얼한 청바지와 티셔츠, 운동화는 더 이상 저에게 멋져 보이지 않았습니다.</td>
</tr>
</table>

예시 답변

리딩 지문에서는 준거 집단의 개념을 논하는데, 이것은 많은 사람들이 존경하고 우러러보며 그들의 행동과 태도를 따라 하고 싶어하는 사람들의 집단이다. 사람들이 나이가 들면서, 준거 집단이 바뀔 수도 있고, 그에 따라 그들의 태도와 행동도 바뀔 것이다.

강의에서 교수는 개인적인 경험을 들려준다. 대학 공부를 시작했을 때, 그는 미대 학생들과 친구가 되었다. 그들은 나이가 많고, 재미있고, 창의적이어서 교수는 그들이 멋지다고 생각했다. 미대생들은 티셔츠와 청바지와 같은 편한 복장을 입었고, 가는 곳마다 그것을 입었다. 그래서 교수도 그렇게 입기 시작했고, 그들과 잘 어울리며 자기 자신이 멋지다고 느꼈다. 나중에 그 교수는 졸업하고 시카고로 이사해서 그곳에 취직했다. 그는 이미 몇 년 동안 회사에서 일해 온 새 직장에서 전도유망한 사람들과 함께 일했다. 그들은 주요 업무를 처리하고 있었고 그것은 매우 인상 깊었다. 때때로 그들은 주말 동안 콘서트나 야구 경기를 위해 모이곤 했는데, 교수는 티셔츠와 청바지를 입는 것에 익숙했기 때문에 그렇게 했다. 하지만, 그는 그의 동료들이 주말에 옷을 차려 입었다는 것을 알아챘다. 남자들은 멋진 바지에 단추를 채우는 셔츠를 입었고 여자들은 멋진 신발과 함께 유행하는 드레스를 입곤 했다. 그들은 교수보다 훨씬 더 멋진 옷을 입었다. 그래서 교수는 동료들이 세련되고 멋지게 옷을 입는다고 생각했다. 그래서 교수는 좀 더 격식을 차린 옷을 입기 시작했다. 교수에게 티셔츠와 청바지는 더 이상 멋있어 보이지 않았다.

이것이 교수가 준거 집단의 개념을 설명하기 위해 사용하는 예이다.

Page.80

연습2

Question 3 of 4

깃대종

인간의 활동은 끊임없이 식물과 동물의 자연 서식지를 위협한다. 그래서 환경 단체들은 이 생물들을 보호하기 위해 끊임없이 노력하고 있다. 그들이 하는 한 가지 특별한 방법은 사람들에게 위협 받는 서식지를 대표하는 특정 생물을 선택하는 것이다. 이 종은 깃대종이라 불리며, 환경 단체들은 대부분 사람들에게 매력적이고 흥미로운 생물을 선택한다. 깃대종의 목적은 위협 받는 환경을 보호하는 데 국민들이 참여할 수 있도록 의식을 높이고 동기를 부여하는 것이다. 깃대종에 대한 그들의 지원은 결국 위협 받는 서식지에 살고 있는 모든 동식물을 보호하게 된다.

강의에 나온 앵무새 마코를 사용하여 깃대종에 대한 개념을 설명하시오.

Now listen to a lecture on this topic in an environmental science class.

One example of a flagship species is the macaw. The Great Green Macaw is a large beautiful bird, known for its gorgeous feathers of mostly green, but a few red and blue feathers. The macaw's habitat is in the South American Rainforest, where a lot of the trees have been cut down. These are the same trees that the macaws rely on for finding food and building its nest. With the continuous cutting down of the trees, the macaws were in trouble. But not just the macaws. Other animals that dwelled in the rainforest, such as birds, bats, and frogs, were also in trouble. When the trees were cut down, these animals also lost their homes, and their numbers greatly decreased.

So a group of people concerned with the situation started to spread the word. They mentioned how the great and beautiful macaw needed help. The group made pamphlets with information about the macaw as well as pictures of the bird to show its beauty. They handed the books out to people in schools and community areas. In a short time, a lot of people contributed in helping out the macaw. People contributed money as well as help the group set up a protected area of land for the birds, where no one was allowed to cut down the trees. The macaws' population started to grow again and other birds, bats, and frogs, also saw a rise in their population.

자연과학 수업 시간에 해당 주제에 관해 이뤄지는 강의를 들으시오.

깃대종의 한 예는 마코 앵무새입니다. Great Green Macaw는 크고 아름다운 새로, 대부분 녹색이고 약간의 빨간색과 파란색이 섞여 있는 멋진 깃털을 가진 것으로 유명합니다. 마코의 서식지는 남아메리카 열대 우림에 있는데, 그곳에서는 많은 나무들이 벌채되었습니다. 이 나무들은 마코들이 먹이를 찾고 둥지를 짓는데 의존하는 나무들과 같습니다. 나무들이 계속 잘려 나가면서 마코들은 곤경에 처했습니다. 그러나 단지 마코뿐만이 아닙니다. 새, 박쥐, 개구리 등 열대 우림에 서식하는 다른 동물들도 곤경에 처했죠. 나무가 벌채됐을 때, 이 동물들도 그들의 서식지를 잃었고, 그 수는 크게 줄어들었습니다.

그래서 그 상황을 걱정하는 한 무리의 사람들이 그 소식을 퍼뜨리기 시작했습니다. 그들은 위대하고 아름다운 마코에게 어떤 도움이 필요한지 말했죠. 그 사람들은 마코에 대한 정보와 함께 그 새의 아름다움을 보여주기 위한 책자를 만들었어요. 그들은 학교와 지역사회에 있는 사람들에게 그 책을 나눠 주었어요. 짧은 시간 안에 많은 사람들이 마코를 돕는 데 기여했어요. 사람들은 이 단체가 새들을 위한 보호 구역을 세우는 것을 도왔을 뿐 아니라 돈도 기부했습니다. 그곳에서는 어느 누구도 나무를 벌채하는 것이 허락되지 않았죠. 마코의 개체 수는 다시 증가하기 시작했고 다른 새, 박쥐, 개구리들도 개체 수가 증가했습니다.

예시 답변

리딩 지문에서는 깃대종 개념에 대해 논의하는데, 이는 대중의 인식을 높이고 위협 받는 서식지를 보호하기 위해 사람들이 행동하도록 동기를 부여하는 데 이용되는 동물이다. 사람들의 지지는 위협 받는 지역에 사는 모든 동식물을 보호하는 결과를 낳는다.

강의에서 교수는 마코의 예를 든다. 마코는 녹색, 빨간색, 파란색의 다채로운 깃털로 유명한 아름답고 큰 앵무새다. 마코는 많은 나무들이 벌채된 남미 열대 우림에 살고 있는데, 그곳은 마코가 음식과 보금자리를 위해 의존하는 많은 나무들이 벌채되었다. 열대 우림에 사는 마코와 다른 동물들은 곤경에 처했다. 다른 새, 박쥐, 나무들도 그 나무에서 살았었다. 나무가 잘려 나가자 그들은 살 곳이 없게 되었고, 개체 수는 줄어들었다. 그래서 사람들은 마코에게 도움이 필요하다는 소식을 퍼뜨리기 시작했다. 그들은 마코에 관한 정보를 담은 책을 만들었고, 이 책자를 학교와 지역 센터에 나누어 주었다. 많은 사람들이 돈을 기부하고, 마코의 안전을 위해 아무도 나무를 자를 수 없도록 보호 지역을 세우는 것을 돕기로 했다. 곧, 마코들의 수는 증가했고, 나중에 다른 동물들이 숲으로 돌아오면서 그 숫자도 증가했다. 따라서 이것이 교수가 깃대종의 개념을 설명하기 위해 사용하는 예이다.

연습3

Question 3 of 4
문화적 지체 오늘날의 현대 세계에서, 기술은 매우 빠르게 변화하고, 때때로 사람들은 발전과 속도를 맞추는데 어려움을 겪는다. 그러므로, 새로운 기술이 나올 때, 사람들은 그 기술에 적응하는 것에 어려움을 겪는다. 이를 문화적 지체라고 하는데, 이는 사람들이 기술 변화에 적응하는 과도기를 뜻한다. 초기에는 신기술에 익숙하지 않고 이해하지 못할 수도 있기 때문에 사람들은 변화에 대해 비관적인 시각을 갖게 될 것이다. 그러나 시간이 흐를수록 그들의 태도는 바뀔 것이고, 새로운 기술을 그들의 삶에 성공적으로 접목시킬 것이다.
전화기의 예를 들어, 그것이 문화적 지체의 개념과 어떻게 관련되는지 설명하시오.

The invention of the telephone was a great stride in technological development. It became faster and much easier to communicate with people, replacing older forms of communication. However, when the telephone was first invented and introduced in the late 19th century, only businesses took advantage of the telephone because they were the only ones that believed that the telephone would benefit them. Most people in the general public did not believe that the newly invented telephone should be used for daily communication. People did not like the idea of not seeing the person's face while talking to them. They also believed that it was rude to call someone, instead of listening to them in person. They believed that the telephone lacked a sense of personal connection that could otherwise be achieved by communicating with the person face to face. Slowly, however, people started to change their minds regarding the telephone. It took a few decades, but in the end, most homes had a telephone and everyone came to rely on them. Talking to someone without contact seemed normal. Friends began to call one another just to chat. After certain telephone etiquette came to be agreed upon, such as not calling someone late at night, using the telephone was no longer regarded as a rude form of communication.	전화기의 발명은 기술 발전에 있어서 큰 진보였다. 구식의 의사소통을 대체하면서 사람들과의 의사소통이 더 빠르고 훨씬 더 쉬워졌다. 그러나 19세기 후반에 전화가 처음 발명되어 도입되었을 때, 회사들만 전화기를 활용했는데 왜냐하면 그들만이 유일하게 전화기가 자신들에게 이점을 줄 것이라 믿었기 때문이다. 대부분의 일반 대중들은 새로 발명된 전화기가 일상에서의 소통을 위해 사용되어야 한다고 믿지 않았다. 사람들은 말을 하는 동안 그 사람의 얼굴을 보지 못한다는 것을 좋아하지 않았다. 또한 그들은 직접 만나 이야기를 듣는 것 대신 누군가에게 전화하는 것이 무례하다고 믿었다. 그들은 전화기에는 그 사람과 직접 대면하고 의사소통 하여 얻을 수 있는 개인적인 관계가 결여되어 있다고 믿었다. 그러나 천천히 사람들은 전화에 대한 생각을 바꾸기 시작했다. 몇 십 년이 걸렸지만 결국 대부분의 가정은 전화기를 가졌고 모두가 그것에 의지하게 되었다. 누군가와 접촉 없이 이야기하는 것이 일반적인 것이 됐다. 친구들은 그저 수다를 떨기 위해 서로 전화를 걸기 시작했다. 밤 늦은 시간에 누군가에게 전화를 하지 않는 등 특정한 전화 예절이 합의된 후, 전화를 사용하는 것은 더 이상 무례한 의사소통의 형태로 간주되지 않았다.

예시 답변

읽기 지문은 사람들이 기술 변화에 적응하기 위해 고군분투하는 시간으로서 문화적 지체 개념을 논한다. 처음에 사람들은 새로운 기술을 이해하지 못하기 때문에 부정적인 태도를 갖게 되겠지만, 일단 그 기술을 그들의 삶에 반영하면 그들의 태도는 바뀔 것이다.

강의에서 교수는 전화기의 예를 든다. 그것은 더 쉽고 빠른 의사소통 방식이었다. 그러나, 전화가 사용이 가능해졌을 때, 회사들만이 전화기가 생산성에 도움이 될 수 있다는 것을 깨닫고 전화를 사용했다. 일반 대중들은 이 전화기가 개인적인 의사소통을 위해 사용되어야 한다고 생각하지 않았다. 사람들은 다른 사람을 보지 않고 말을 듣는 것을 좋아하지 않았다. 또 개인적인 관계를 맺는 것으로 여겨지는 방문 대신 전화를 거는 것은 무례한 것이라고 생각했다.

그러나 사람들은 점차 전화에 대한 생각을 바꾸었다. 약 30년이 걸렸지만, 결국 대부분의 가정이 전화기를 가지게 되었다. 보지 않고 사람들과 대화하는 것이 더 일반적인 일이 되었다. 사람들은 그저 재미로 수다를 떨기 위해 서로에게 전화를 했다. 밤에 누군가에게 전화하지 않는 것과 같은 특정한 예절에 모든 사람들이 동의한 후에는, 전화를 사용하는 것은 더 이상 무례한 일이 아니게 되었다.

결론적으로, 이것이 교수가 문화적 지체의 개념을 설명하기 위해 사용하는 예다.

Page.86

연습4

Question 3 of 4

착생 식물

남아메리카의 열대 우림에서, 나무의 윗층에서 생산되는 캐노피는 매우 **빽빽할 수** 있고, 그래서 그 아래의 땅에서는 식물이 거의 자랄 수 없다.

그럼에도 불구하고, 식물들은 특별한 생존 방법을 개발함으로써 이러한 그늘진 땅에서의 삶에 적응해 왔다. 예를 들어, 착생 식물이라고 불리는 식물의 종은 성장을 위한 기반으로 숙주 식물을 사용한다. 착생 식물은 숙주 나무에서 자라지만 나무에서 어떠한 영양분도 흡수하지 않는다. 착생 식물은 나무 위 30~40m 지점에 붙어 햇빛을 쬐지만 땅으로부터 영양분을 얻는 것은 아니다. 그래서 착생 식물은 이 장애를 극복하기 위한 메커니즘을 진화시켜왔다.

항아리 식물의 예를 이용하여, 어떻게 착생 식물이 열대 우림에서의 삶에 적응했는지 설명하시오.

Now listen to a lecture from a biology class.

A good example of an epiphyte plant is the urn plant. Urn plants are found in the Amazon rainforests. They wrap their roots around the branches of the trees, sometimes even wrapping around the upper levels of the trunks. They use the trees as support, which help them to dwell in the higher levels of the trees, near the canopy, so that they can get plenty of sunlight.

The urn plant has a unique shape. The name of this plant comes from the leaves that form a urn or a bowl, so that it can store water. The urn plants have long and spiky leaves. The leaves are tightly rolled into a cone-shape, like a funnel. The flower of the urn plant is held by a single stem in the center.

The shape of the leaves form a bowl so that when rainwater falls on the leaves, it slides down into the bowl so that it can be stored. So the urn plant's unique shape help retrieve and store water.

The bowl shaped leaves also help the urn plant to get other nutrients. Insects, dead leaves, and other debris from the rainforest land on the leaves and get washed down into the saved water. Slowly, the ingredients decompose and the mixture becomes a nitrogen rich source mixed with water. So the water supply also contains a nutritious supplement which helps the urn plant survive in the rainforest.

이제 생물학 수업의 강의를 들으시오.

착생 식물의 좋은 예는 항아리 식물입니다. 항아리 식물은 아마존 열대 우림에서 발견됩니다. 그들은 나무 가지를 자신들의 뿌리로 감싸고, 때로는 나무 줄기의 윗부분을 감싸기도 합니다. 그들은 나무를 지지대로 사용하는데, 이것은 그들이 캐노피 근처의 나무의 높은 위치에서 살 수 있도록 도와주어, 그들이 충분한 햇빛을 받을 수 있게 해 줍니다.

항아리 식물은 독특한 모양을 하고 있습니다. 이 식물의 이름은 물을 저장할 수 있는 항아리나 그릇 형태의 잎에서 유래합니다. 항아리 식물은 길고 뾰족한 잎을 가지고 있습니다. 잎은 깔때기처럼 원뿔 모양으로 촘촘히 말려 있죠. 항아리의 꽃은 중앙에 있는 하나의 줄기에 꽂혀 있습니다. 잎의 모양은 그릇 형태로, 빗물이 잎에 떨어지면 그릇 속으로 물이 미끄러져 내려가 저장됩니다. 그래서 항아리 식물의 독특한 모양은 물을 회수하고 저장하는 것을 돕습니다.

그릇 모양의 잎은 또한 항아리 식물이 다른 영양분을 얻는 것을 돕습니다. 열대 우림 지대의 곤충, 낙엽, 그리고 다른 잔해들이 잎 위에 내려앉아 저장된 물이 있는 곳으로 씻겨 내려갑니다. 천천히 성분들이 분해되고, 혼합물은 물과 혼합되어 질소가 풍부한 공급원이 됩니다. 그래서 물에는 항아리 식물이 열대 우림에서 생존할 수 있도록 도와주는 영양 보충물 또한 포함되어 있습니다.

예시 답변

읽기 지문에서는 숙주 식물을 성장의 발판으로 사용하는 착생 식물의 개념을 논한다. 나무에서 자라는 동안, 착생 식물은 그 나무에서 영양분을 전혀 취하지 않는다.

강의에서 교수는 항아리 식물을 예로 든다. 항아리 식물은 나무의 가지나 줄기에 뿌리를 감는다. 그들은 지지대로 나무를 사용하며 이것은 그들이 나무들 사이에서 햇빛을 받을 수 있는 높은 곳에 살 수 있게 해준다. 이 항아리 식물은 독특한 형태를 가지고 있다.

그것의 잎은 물을 저장하기 위해 항아리나 그릇 모양을 만든다. 잎은 길고 뾰족하며 말린 원뿔 모양이다. 그 꽃들은 한 줄기에 꽂혀 있다. 나뭇잎에 빗물이 모이면, 그것은 보관할 그릇으로 굴러 떨어진다. 독특한 그릇 모양은 식물이 영양분을 모으는 데 도움을 준다.

곤충, 죽은 나뭇잎, 그리고 다른 잔해들은 나뭇잎 위에 떨어져서 저장된 물이 있는 곳으로 씻겨 내려가고, 그곳에서 분해된다. 생성된 화학 물질은 질소가 풍부하고, 그 생성된 물은 마치 액체 비료와 같다.

따라서, 이것은 교수가 착생 식물의 개념을 설명하기 위해 사용하는 예다.

연습5

Question 3 of 4

무리 지능

어떤 종류의 곤충들은 떼라고 불리는 큰 무리를 지어 산다. 떼는 수천 마리의 곤충들이 함께 사는 것이다. 곤충은 떼의 일원이 되어 복잡한 행동을 함으로써 복잡한 임무를 수행할 수 있다. 곤충 떼들은 개별 곤충의 행동보다 훨씬 진보된 복잡한 행동을 보인다. 곤충 떼 속에서 보이는 이러한 집단 행동을 무리 지능이라고 한다. 무리 지능은 각 곤충이 단순한 본능적인 행동을 함으로써 생기는데, 이것은 다른 무리 구성원들에 의해 반복되어 복잡한 행동을 낳는다. 이 복잡한 행동을 통해 곤충 떼들은 개별 곤충들이 성취하기 불가능한 임무를 수행할 수 있다.

강의에서 나온 예시가 어떻게 무리 지능의 개념을 설명하는지 진술하시오.

Now listen to a lecture from a biology class.

A great example of swarm intelligence can be seen by ants. Ants live together in large groups called colonies. Normally, the ants would move together to get to a food source. Sometimes, the ants would encounter an obstacle in their path, which would inhibit them from getting to the food.

For instance, if a group of ants are marching on a tree, to look for food on a branch, they may encounter an obstacle within the tree. The tree branch they are walking on may have a wide gap between the next tree branch with the food. If the ants were to have been alone, it would have been impossible to get to the other side of the branch. But with swarm intelligence, it becomes possible. One ant would reach to the end of the branch the group is on. It would hold onto the tip of the branch with its hind legs and stretch its body towards the open gap. A second ant will climb over the first ant, latch its back leg to the first ant's front legs and it too will stretch its body over the gap. This action will be repeated by the other ants until enough ants have been connected to form a bridge between the gap. Amazing isn't it? The bridged ants will hold this position, allowing the rest of the ants to cross over them, getting to the food on the other side of the branch.

이제 생물학 수업에서 이 주제에 대한 강의를 들어보자.

무리 지능의 훌륭한 예는 개미들에게서 볼 수 있습니다. 개미는 군집이라 불리는 큰 무리를 지어 삽니다. 보통, 개미들은 식량을 얻기 위해 함께 움직입니다. 때때로 개미들은 길에서 장애물을 마주치곤 했는데, 그것은 그들이 먹이에 도달하는 것을 막습니다.

예를 들어, 한 무리의 개미들이 나뭇가지에서 먹이를 찾기 위해 나무 위를 행진하고 있다면, 그들은 나무 안에서 장애물에 부딪힐 수 있습니다. 그들이 걸어가는 나뭇가지와 먹이가 있는 다음 가지와의 간격은 넓을 수 있습니다. 만약 개미들이 혼자였다면 저편의 나뭇가지까지 가는 것은 불가능했을 것입니다. 하지만 무리 지능으로, 그것은 가능해집니다.

개미 한 마리가 그 집단이 타고 있는 나뭇가지 끝에 닿을 것입니다. 그 개미는 뒷다리로 나뭇가지 끝을 잡고 열린 틈으로 몸을 뻗겠죠. 두 번째 개미는 첫 번째 개미를 기어올라, 첫 번째 개미의 앞다리에 뒷다리를 걸치고, 그 틈새로 몸을 뻗을 것입니다. 이 행동은 틈새 사이에 다리를 놓을 수 있을 정도로 개미가 충분히 연결될 때까지 다른 개미들에 의해 반복될 것입니다. 놀랍지 않습니까? 다리를 만든 개미들은 이 자세를 유지하여 나머지 개미들이 그 위를 건너 나뭇가지 반대편에 있는 먹이로 가도록 만들어 줄 것입니다.

예시 답변

읽기 지문에서는 무리 지능의 개념을 논하는데, 그것은 각 곤충이 단순한 본능적 행동을 취하고 그것이 다른 곤충들에 의해 반복되어 복잡한 행동을 하게 되는 것을 말한다. 무리 지능으로 곤충들은 개별 곤충들이 성취할 수 없는 임무를 수행할 수 있다.

강의에서 교수는 개미의 예를 든다. 개미는 집단으로 산다. 그들은 식량을 얻기 위해 함께 움직인다. 때때로 개미들은 장애물에 부딪힐 수도 있다. 한 무리의 개미들이 나뭇가지에 앉아 먹이를 찾는다면, 그들은 가지 끝에 다다를 수 있을 것이다. 그들이 타고 있는 나뭇가지 끝과 먹이가 있는 다른 나뭇가지 사이에는 넓은 공간이 있을 수 있다. 이 개미들은 혼자서 다른 쪽으로 갈 수 없을 것이다.

그래서 앞으로 일어날 일은 개미 한 마리가 나뭇가지 끝으로 가서 뒷다리로 나뭇가지를 잡고 있는 것이다. 그러면 다른 개미 하나가 첫 번째 개미 위를 걸어가서 첫 번째 개미의 뒷다리로 잡고 몸을 뻗을 것이다. 두 가지 사이에 다리가 놓일 때까지 다른 개미들도 같은 행동을 할 것이다. 연결된 개미들은 다른 개미들이 건너가 먹이에 닿는 동안 그 자세를 유지할 것이다. 따라서 이것이 교수가 무리 지능의 개념을 설명하기 위해 사용하는 예다.

Chapter04
Q4 Lecture

Page.96

Q4. 강의

스피킹 영역의 마지막 문제에서, 당신은 학문적인 주제에 대한 강의를 듣게 될 것이다. 답변을 위해 그 강의를 요약해야 한다. 답변을 준비할 시간은 20초, 답변을 녹음할 시간은 60초가 주어진다.

문제는 어떻게 제시되는가:

> 강의에서 핵심 내용과 예를 들어, 상어와 돌고래가 어떻게 해서 성공적인 사냥꾼으로 진화했는지에 대해 논하시오.

> 강의의 핵심 내용과 예시를 사용하여 지역 대학의 두 가지 장점을 설명하시오.

> 토론의 핵심 내용과 예시를 사용하여 탄수화물이 적은 식단이 개인의 건강에 어떤 영향을 미칠 수 있는지 설명하시오.

왜 이 문항에서 낮은 점수를 받는가?

수험생늘이 이 분제에서 낮은 점수를 받는 데는 여러 이유가 있다.

1) **잘린 응답.** 60초에서 응답이 끊기는 불완전한 응답을 하는 것은 더 낮은 점수를 받는다는 것에 유의해야 한다. 단절된 응답보다 55초간 답변을 하고, 5초간 침묵하는 것이 좋다.

2) **세부 사항 부족.** 이 답변은 리스닝을 얼마나 잘 요약할 수 있느냐에 기반한다. 강의를 들을 때는 반드시 잘 메모하고, 답변에 그 세부 사항을 언급하라.

3) **언급되지 않았거나 잘못 표현된 정보.** 때때로 수험생들은 리딩과 리스닝에 언급되지 않은 정보를 포함하게 된다. 그들은 이 문제에 관한 배경 지식 혹은 개인적인 경험을 가지고 있거나, 정보를 잘못 들었을 수도 있기 때문에 이렇게 하는 경향이 있다. 리스닝에 언급된 정보만 포함시켜라. 또한, 정보가 잘못 주어질 수 있다. 언급된 내용을 이해하도록 최선을 다해야 한다.

4) **조직되지 않은 답변.** 두 가지 핵심 정보가 주어진다면, 당신의 답변은 이를 분명하게 구분해야 한다. 이 질문 유형의 말하기 템플릿을 따르라.

5) **문법 오용.** 놀랍게도, 문법은 점수를 감점시키는 가장 큰 측면은 아니다. 기억하라, 토플 시험을 보는 대부분의 학생들은 원어민이 아닌 영어 사용자들이기 때문에 그들의 문법은 완벽하지 않을 것이다. 그래도 문법 실수가 너무 많으면 점수가 낮아진다.

6) **말이 너무 부드럽거나 느리다.** 당신의 스피킹 답변은 사람 또는 컴퓨터에 의해 등급이 매겨진다. 목소리가 너무 부드럽거나 느려서 컴퓨터가 알아듣지 못하면 내용이 완벽해도 낮은 점수를 받는다.

단계별 답변 방법:

1) 강의를 들어라. 강의는 한 번만 재생되므로 체계적으로 메모하라.

2) 20초 안에 답변을 준비하라. 이때, 당신은 메모를 정리하거나 답변 연습을 할 수 있다.

3) 60초안에 답변하라.

노트 테이킹:

정리된 필기를 하는 것이 중요하므로 스피킹 섹션을 시작하기 전에 필기를 준비하는 것이 좋다. 이 질문 유형에 대한 메모는 다음과 같은 방식으로 정리되어야 한다.

Main idea:
Lecture's point 1:
Detail:
Lecture's point 2:
Detail:

리스닝 섹션

그 강의는 학문적인 추세에 관한 구체적인 예나 주제에 대해 토론할 것이다. 강의에서는 대부분 두 가지 핵심 내용을 언급할 것이다. 그러나 때때로 교수는 일반적인 주제를 뒷받침하는 동안 개인적인 경험을 말할 수도 있다. 필기를 철저히 하라. 내용을 이해하는 데 어려움이 있더라도 듣는 단어를 적어 보아라. 이 문항의 요점은 이해가 아니라 요약하는 것이다.

강의는 2분 이내로 끝날 것이다. 가능한 한 많은 정보를 기록하려는 것이 필수적이다. 여기에는 사물을 묘사하는 데 사용된 형용사뿐만 아니라 이름과 숫자도 포함된다. 요약하면 할수록 더 많은 점수를 얻게 된다는 것을 기억하라.

흥미로운 점은 강의의 주요 아이디어가 실제로 문제에 명시되어 있다는 점이다. 그래서 강의를 듣고 있을 때는 주요 아이디어를 적을 필요가 없고, 예시나 요점에만 초점을 맞추면 된다.

강의의 주요 아이디어 예시:

> 강의의 핵심 내용과 예를 들어, 상어와 돌고래가 어떻게 해서 성공적인 사냥꾼으로 진화했는지에 대해 논하라.
>
> 이 강의의 핵심 내용은 상어와 돌고래가 어떻게 해서 성공적인 사냥꾼이 되었는가 하는 것이다.

> 강연에서 나온 핵심 내용과 예시를 사용하여 지역 대학의 두 가지 장점을 설명하라.
>
> 강의의 핵심 내용은 지역 대학의 두 가지 장점을 설명한다.

> 토론의 핵심 내용과 예시를 사용하여 탄수화물이 적은 식단이 개인의 건강에 어떤 영향을 미칠 수 있는지 설명하라.
>
> 그 강의의 핵심 내용은 저탄수화물 식단이 사람의 건강에 어떤 영향을 미칠 수 있는지에 있다.

생물학 수업을 들으시오,

많은 동물들이 땅 밑에서 산다. 여기에는 벌레와 같은 작은 유기체부터 더 큰 포유류까지 포함한다. 지하에 사는 것의 가장 큰 이점은 땅 위에 사는 포식자들로부터 보호하는 것이다. 하지만 지하에 사는 것은 땅 속 생물 그들 자신에게도 도전이다. 다행히 지하에 사는 동물들은 도전에 맞서기 위해 신체적 특성을 적응시켰다. 지하에 사는 것의 가장 큰 문제 중 하나는 흙을 통해 이동하는 것이다. 또 다른 문제는 흙 속에서 이동할 때, 신체의 취약한 부분을 토양으로부터 보호하는 것이다.

흙을 통해 움직이는 것은 땅 위를 움직이는 것과 전혀 다르다. 토양이 두껍고 단단하기 때문에, 지하에 사는 동물들은 토양 속을 더 효율적으로 이동할 수 있는 특징을 진화 시켰다. 예를 들어, 두더지는 흙을 파는데 도움이 되는 긴 발톱과 함께 엄청나게 넓고 강한 앞발을 가지고 있다. 두더지의 앞발은 삽과 같은 역할을 해서 지하로 이동하는 것을 돕는다. 긴 발톱은 흙으로 파고 들어 흙을 부드럽게 하고 넓은 발은 흙을 뒤로 던지며 두더지는 앞으로 나아갈 것이다. 긴 발톱을 가진 튼튼한 넓은 발은 두더지가 믿을 수 없는 속도로 지하에서 움직일 수 있도록 도와준다.

비록 지하로 이동하는 것이 그 곳에 사는 동물들에게는 쉬울 수 있지만, 작은 돌과 모래 조각들이 포유류의 눈과 같이 동물들의 민감한 부분에 박힐 수 있다. 그래서 동물들은 이것을 막기 위해 다시 적응했다. 다시 두더지의 예를 들어보자. 우선 두더지는 털이 달린 보호막인 얇은 피부에 가려진 작은 눈을 가지고 있다. 털은 바위와 모래로부터 눈을 보호한다. 두더지가 머리를 앞으로 하고 흙 속을 움직이면 바위와 모래가 막의 털과 접촉하게 된다. 그러면 입자들은 막에 걸리지 않고 미끄러져 나갈 것이다. 두더지의 눈은 이런 식으로 보호된다.

이 강의는 두 가지 핵심 내용을 제시한다. 이것은 스피킹 템플릿에서 "To begin with "와 "Furthermore"라는 문구를 언급함으로써 당신의 답변을 두 지점으로 나누어야 한다는 것을 의미한다.

기억하라, 모든 세부 사항들이 중요하다. 당신의 메모에는 흙의 특징(두껍고 단단한 것), 두더지의 앞발(매우 넓고 강한 것), 두더지가 지하를 통해 이동하는 순서 등이 포함되어야 한다.

문제 :

> 두더지의 예시를 사용하여, 땅 속 적응의 두 가지 유형에 대하여 설명하라.

예시 답변

이 강의에서 교수는 두 가지 다른 유형의 땅 속 적응에 대해 설명한다.

우선, 동물들은 땅 속에서, 흙을 통해 움직이는 것에 적응해야 한다. 흙을 헤치고 움직이는 것은 흙이 두껍고 단단하기 때문에 땅 위에서 움직이는 것과 다르다. 두껍고 빽빽하기에 지하에 사는 동물들은 흙 속을 움직이는 것을 돕는 특징을 진화시켰다. 예를 들어, 두더지는 넓고 매우 강한 발과 발톱을 가지고 있다. 앞발은 흙을 파낼 수 있는 삽처럼 쓰인다. 두더지의 발톱은 흙을 파서 퍼 내고, 넓은 발은 몸을 움직일 수 있도록 두더지 뒤로 흙을 던진다. 이 삽과 같은 발은 두더지가 흙 속을 빠르게 움직이도록 돕는다.

게다가, 동물들은 땅 속에서 이동하는 동안 몸의 취약한 부분을 보호해야 한다.

예를 들어, 두더지는 작은 눈을 가지고 있고 그들은 털이 있는 보호막인 얇은 피부로 덮여 있다. 털은 먼지 입자로부터 눈을 보호한다. 그래서 두더지가 흙 사이로 이동하는 동안 흙은 털이 풍성한 막과 접촉하게 된다. 입자가 미끄러져 지나가면, 민감한 눈은 보호된다.

그러므로 이 두 가지가 서로 다른 형태의 땅 속 적응이다.

Page.103

연습1

Question 4 of 4
파리지옥과 끈끈이주걱의 예를 이용하여 식충 식물이 그들의 영양분을 섭취하는 두 가지 방법을 설명하라

Listen to a lecture in a biology class. Plants, like animals, need to take in nutrients to survive, thrive and grow. Humans and animals get nutrients from the food they eat. Most plants absorb their nutrients from the soil using their extensive root systems. However, there are some plants that do not get their nutrients from the soil. This is because the soil where they live does not contain much nutrition. So they get their nutrients from insects by trapping and digesting them. These plants that catch insects are called carnivorous plants. Carnivorous plants catch insects in different ways, using two different types of trapping mechanisms. These are active traps and passive traps. A good example of a plant that uses active traps are the Venus flytrap. The Venus flytrap will actually move to catch its prey. Its specialized leaves are hinged so that the two halves of the leaves can open and close. It acts like a mouth to catch insects. There is sweet nectar on the leaves to attract insects. When the insects land on the leaves, the leaves spring shut. This is an active trap. The insect triggers the leaves to close, trapping the insect in between the leaves. The Venus flytrap then starts to digest the insect and gets its nutrients. Other carnivorous plants use passive traps to capture its prey. These plants do not have moving parts to trap the prey. For example, the sundew plant uses passive traps. The sundew plant also produces a sweet nectar to trap insects. Its leaves are covered with little hair that secretes nectar. So how does this plant trap the insect? Well, when an insect lands on a sundew plant to eat the nectar, the hairs on the leaves trap the insects. This is due to a sticky substance that is created by the hairs, alongside the sweet nectar. So an insect will get glued to the hair and will not be able to escape. Then, the sundew plant will be able to digest the insect and absorb its nutrients.	생물학 시간의 강의를 들으시오. 식물도 동물과 마찬가지로 생존하고, 번성하고, 자라기 위해 영양분을 섭취해야 합니다. 인간과 동물은 우리가 먹는 음식으로부터 영양분을 얻습니다. 대부분의 식물들은 그들의 광범위한 뿌리를 이용하여 토양으로부터 영양분을 흡수합니다. 그러나 흙에서 영양분을 얻지 못하는 식물도 있습니다. 그들이 사는 토양에 영양분이 많지 않기 때문이죠. 그래서 그들은 곤충을 잡아 소화시키는 방법으로 곤충으로부터 영양분을 얻습니다. 곤충을 잡는 이러한 식물은 식충 식물이라고 불러요. 식충 식물은 두 가지 다른 종류의 포획 메커니즘을 사용하여 곤충을 잡습니다. 이 메커니즘은 능동형 덫과 수동형 덫입니다. 능동형 덫을 사용하는 식물의 좋은 예는 파리지옥입니다. 파리지옥은 먹이를 잡기 위해 실제로 움직이죠. 그것의 특화된 잎에는 경첩이 달려 있어서 반 쪽짜리 잎 두 개가 열리고 닫힐 수 있습니다. 그것은 곤충을 잡는 입처럼 행동합니다. 잎 표면에는 달콤한 과즙이 있어 곤충을 유혹하죠. 곤충들이 잎에 앉으면, 잎 스프링이 닫힙니다. 이것이 능동형 덫이예요. 그 식물은 나뭇잎을 닫아 그 곤충을 잎 사이에 가두어 놓습니다. 그리고 나서 파리지옥은 곤충을 소화하고 영양분을 얻기 시작합니다. 다른 식충 식물들은 먹이를 잡기 위해 수동형 덫을 사용합니다. 이 식물들은 먹잇감을 가두기 위한 움직이는 부분이 없어요. 예를 들어, 끈끈이주걱은 수동형 덫을 사용합니다. 끈끈이주걱 또한 곤충들을 가두기 위해 달콤한 과즙을 생산합니다. 그 잎은 과즙을 분비하는 작은 털로 덮여 있습니다. 그렇다면 이 식물은 어떻게 곤충을 가두는 걸까요? 아마도, 곤충이 과즙을 먹기 위해 끈끈이주걱에 앉았을 때, 잎에 난 털이 곤충들을 가둘 것입니다. 이것은 달콤한 과즙과 함께 털에 의해 생성되는 끈적끈적한 물질 때문입니다. 그래서 곤충은 털에 달라붙게 되어 도망칠 수 없을 겁니다. 그러면, 끈끈이주걱은 그 곤충을 소화하고 영양분을 흡수할 수 있습니다.

예시 답변

교수는 강연에서 파리지옥과 끈끈이주걱을 예로 들어 식충 식물이 영양분을 얻는 두 가지 방법을 설명한다.

우선 교수는 능동형 덫에 대해 언급한다. 이것의 좋은 예는 파리지옥이다. 식물의 일부분이 먹이를 잡기 위해 움직인다. 그 잎은 가운데 경첩이 달려 있다는 점에서 특이하다. 반 쪽짜리 잎 두 개가 벌레를 잡기 위해 입처럼 열리고 닫힌다. 잎 위에는 곤충을 유혹하는 달콤한 과즙이 있다. 곤충들이 잎에 앉으면, 그들은 딱 닫힌다. 그러므로 그것이 능동형 덫이다. 잎이 닫히고 포획틀을 형성하여 곤충을 가두어 버린다. 그리고 나서 파리지옥은 곤충들을 소화하고 영양분을 얻는다.

게다가, 교수는 일부 식물들은 움직이는 부분이 없는 수동형 덫을 사용한다고 말한다. 교수는 끈끈이주걱에 대해 언급한다. 그것은 곤충을 유인하는 달콤한 과즙도 만든다. 잎에는 과즙을 분비하는 작은 털이 가득하다. 곤충들이 과즙을 얻기 위해 잎에 앉을 때, 잎의 털은 끈적끈적한 접착제 같은 물질을 생산하여 곤충들을 가두어 버린다. 그래서 곤충들은 꼼짝 못하게 되고 도망칠 수 없게 된다. 그러면 끈끈이주걱은 곤충을 소화하고 영양분을 흡수할 것이다.

그러므로, 이것이 교수가 식충 식물이 영양분을 얻는 두 가지 방법을 설명하기 위해 사용하는 예들이다.

Page.106

연습2

Question 4 of 4
강의에 나온 예를 들어, 소설가가 사용할 수 있는 두 가지 유형의 내레이터를 설명하라.

<table>
<tr>
<td>

Listen to part of a lecture from a literature class.
When authors of fictional books write their stories, they have many decisions to make. One of these important decisions is how they are going to narrate, or tell the story. This refers to which point of view or perspective they will tell the story from. The authors need to choose a person or a voice to tell the story and depending on who is telling the story, it can greatly affect the reader as they read the story.
One of these narrators can be an objective narrator. This type of narrator describes the characters in the story in what they do or say. But that is all. For example, in a story with a man and a woman about to take a trip, an objective narrator will only include information, such as what the man and the woman say to each other and what they do. They will get on the train, take their seat, and look out the window. That would be all the information that is provided. This sort of narration will force the reader to make guesses and interpret the events. Readers will try to guess the meaning of the conversations and the actions.
Another narrator that the author can use is the omniscient narrator. This type of narrator knows everything about the characters. So in the same story of the man and woman traveling, the omniscient narrator will describe what the characters are saying and behaving, but the narrator will also tell what the characters are thinking. For instance, the couple is going on a trip to visit a friend of the man's, and the omniscient narrator will narrate the man's thoughts, that he is nervous about meeting his friend whom he hasn't seen for a long time and whether or not his wife will like the friend. So an omniscient narrator provides more information and answers any questions the readers might have regarding the characters or their actions.

</td>
<td>

문학 수업 강의의 일부를 들으시오
소설가들이 이야기를 쓸 때, 그들은 많은 결정을 내려야 합니다. 이 중요한 결정들 중 하나는 그들이 어떻게 이야기를 서술하거나 말할 것인가입니다. 이것은 그들이 어떤 시점과 관점을 가지고 이야기를 전개할 것인지를 의미합니다. 작가들은 이야기를 들려줄 인물이나 목소리를 선택할 필요가 있으며, 누가 이야기를 들려주느냐에 따라 이야기를 읽는 독자들에게 큰 영향을 미칠 수 있습니다.
이들 내레이터 중 한 명은 객관적 내레이터가 될 수 있습니다. 이런 유형의 내레이터는 이야기의 등장인물들이 행동하거나 말하는 것을 묘사합니다. 하지만 그것이 전부입니다. 예를 들어, 여행을 막 떠나려는 한 남녀의 이야기에서 객관적 내레이터는 남자와 여자가 서로에게 하는 말, 그리고 그들의 행동과 같은 정보만을 포함할 겁니다. 그들은 기차를 타고 자리에 앉아 창 밖을 내다보겠죠. 그것이 제공되는 모든 정보입니다. 이런 종류의 내레이션은 독자들이 사건을 추측하고 해석하도록 할 겁니다. 독자들은 대화와 행동의 의미를 추측하려고 노력할 것이고요.
저자가 사용할 수 있는 또 다른 내레이터는 전지적 내레이터입니다. 이런 유형의 내레이터는 등장인물에 대한 모든 것을 알고 있습니다. 그래서 남녀가 여행하는 똑같은 이야기에서 전지적 내레이터는 등장인물들이 말하고 행동하는 것을 묘사할 것이지만, 등장인물들이 어떤 생각을 하고 있는지도 말할 겁니다. 예를 들어, 그 커플은 남자 쪽 친구를 방문하기 위해 여행을 갈 것이고, 전지적 내레이터는 그 남자가 오랫동안 보지 못한 친구를 만나는 것에 대해 긴장하고 있는 것, 자기 아내가 그 친구를 좋아할 것인지 싫어할 것인지에 대한 생각을 이야기할 겁니다. 따라서 전지적 내레이터는 더 많은 정보와 독자들이 등장인물이나 그들의 행동에 대해 가질 수 있는 모든 질문에 대한 답을 제공합니다.

</td>
</tr>
</table>

예시 답변

교수는 이 강의에서 소설가가 사용할 수 있는 두 가지 유형의 내레이터에 대해 논한다.

먼저, 교수는 객관적 내레이터에 대해 이야기한다. 객관적 내레이터는 이야기 속의 등장인물이 하는 일, 그리고 말하는 것을 묘사하는 것이 전부다. 예를 들어, 만약 어떤 이야기에서 한 남자와 한 여자가 여행을 떠나려고 하는 것을 보여 준다면, 객관적 내레이터는 등장인물들이 서로에게 말하는 것과 그들의 행동에 대한 정보만을 줄 것이다. 이것은 독자들이 사건을 해석하고 그 행동과 대화가 의미하는 정보를 채우도록 만든다.

교수가 논하는 또 다른 내레이터는 전지적 내레이터다. 여기 내레이터는 등장인물에 대한 모든 것을 알고 있다. 남녀가 여행하는 같은 시나리오에서 독자들은 등장인물이 무엇을 하고 말하는지 알 뿐만 아니라, 등장인물이 어떤 생각을 하는지도 알 수 있다. 예를 들어, 그 커플은 남자 쪽 친구를 방문할 것이고, 독자는 그가 오랫동안 친구를 만나지 못했기 때문에 긴장하고 있다는 것과 그의 아내가 그 친구를 좋아할지에 대해 걱정하고 있다는 생각을 알게 된다. 그래서 전지적 내레이터는 더 많은 정보를 제공하고 독자들이 가질 수 있는 질문에 대답할 것이다.

그러므로, 이것들이 소설의 저자가 사용할 수 있는 두 종류의 내레이터이다.

Page.109

연습3

Question 4 of 4
강의의 요점과 예시를 사용하여, 풍화 작용이 일어나는 두 가지 방법을 설명하라

Listen to a lecture in a geology class. Rocks on the surface of our planet are constantly exposed to the forces of nature, like air and water. However, temperature changes and living organisms also affect the rocks. This exposure to the forces of the environment can actually cause huge rocks to break down into smaller pieces of rocks. When rocks break down from forces of nature, it is called weathering. Let's discuss two ways in which weathering occurs. First, rocks are frequently exposed to water. In cold and wet environments, rocks can break apart from the freezing of water inside of them. This happens because when water freezes, it expands. Over a period of time, this can cause rocks to break. If a rock has a small crack or a hole, water from rain can get into it. At night when the temperature drops, the water inside the rock freezes. The expanding water pushes the rock on all sides. When this happens repeatedly, the crack becomes larger and breaks up the rock. Second, weathering can occur due to plant growth. A plant seed may get blown into a crack or a hole in a rock and take root. The roots will grow down into the rock. The roots will cause fracture in the rock, like the ones you see with rocks and the roots of trees growing over them. There is enough dirt in the crack or the hole to allow the tree to grow. Over the years, the tree root extends down the rock in search of nutrients and water. The roots will grow larger as time passes, and the cracks in the rock will also get bigger, which will cause the rock to weather.	지질학 수업의 강의를 들으시오. 우리 행성의 표면에 있는 바위는 공기나 물과 같은 자연의 힘에 끊임없이 노출됩니다. 하지만, 변화하는 온도와 살아있는 유기체들도 그 바위에 영향을 미칩니다. 환경의 힘에 대한 이러한 노출은 실제로 거대한 바위가 더 작은 바위로 부서지게 할 수 있습니다. 바위가 자연의 힘으로부터 부서질 때, 그것을 풍화라고 부릅니다. 풍화 현상이 일어나는 두 가지 방법에 대해 토론해 봅시다. 첫 번째로, 바위는 자주 물에 노출됩니다. 춥고 습한 환경에서는 바위 안에 있는 물이 얼어서 바위가 부서질 수 있어요. 물은 얼면 팽창하기 때문이죠. 일정 시간 동안, 이것은 바위가 부서지는 원인이 될 수 있습니다. 만약 바위에 작은 균열이나 구멍이 있다면, 빗물이 바위에 들어갈 수 있어요. 기온이 떨어지는 밤에는 바위 안의 물이 얼어 버립니다. 팽창하는 물이 바위의 사방으로 압력을 가하죠. 이런 일이 반복되면 균열이 커지고 바위가 부서집니다. 두 번째, 식물의 성장으로 인해 풍화 작용이 발생할 수 있습니다. 식물의 씨앗은 바위 틈이나 구멍으로 날아가 뿌리를 내릴 수 있어요. 그 뿌리는 바위 안으로 자랄 겁니다. 이는 마치 나무의 뿌리가 바위 위에 자라는 것처럼 그 뿌리는 바위에 균열을 일으킵니다. 금이나 구멍 안에 충분한 흙이 있어서 나무가 자랄 수 있도록 해주죠. 수 년에 걸쳐, 나무 뿌리는 영양분과 물을 찾아 바위를 타고 뻗어 내려갑니다. 시간이 지날수록 뿌리는 더 커지게 되고, 바위의 갈라진 틈도 더 커지면 바위는 풍화됩니다.

예시 답변

이 강의에서 교수는 풍화 작용이 일어나는 두 가지 방법을 설명한다.

우선, 바위는 종종 물에 노출된다. 추운 환경에서 바위는 그 안에 있는 물이 얼어서 부서질 수 있다. 물이 얼면 팽창하고 시간이 지나면 풍화 작용으로 이어질 수 있다. 바위에 작은 구멍이나 균열이 생기면 그 틈으로 빗물이 떨어진다. 그러면 기온이 떨어지는 밤에는 물이 얼게 될 것이다. 팽창하는 얼음은 갈라진 틈의 면들을 밀어서 틈이 더 커지게 할 것이다. 이런 일이 반복되면 균열이 더 커져서 바위 조각이 부서지게 된다.

게다가, 풍화 작용은 식물의 성장에 의해서도 일어날 수 있다. 식물의 씨앗이 바위 틈으로 날아가면 안 쪽에 뿌리를 내리고 뿌리가 바위 안으로 자란다. 그 식물의 뿌리는 바위를 부술 것이다. 이것의 좋은 예는 나무가 바위 위에서 자라고 있을 때이다. 나무가 자라면서 나무 뿌리는 물과 영양분을 찾아 바위 틈으로 뻗어 나간다. 시간이 흐르면서 뿌리가 점점 커지고 넓어지게 되고, 이것은 바위의 균열을 더 커지게 하고 부술 것이다.

결론적으로, 이것이 풍화 작용이 일어나는 두 가지 방법이다.

Page.112

연습4

Question 4 of 4
강의의 요점과 예시들을 사용하여 제품의 용기가 고객에게 어필할 수 있도록 설계되는 두 가지 방법을 설명하시오.

Listen to a lecture in a geology class. When consumers walk into a store to purchase a product, they are not just buying the product itself. They are also purchasing the container the item comes in. So the design of the container is important. So important, that it can become the deciding factor when buyers decide which brand to buy. Today we will discuss a few ways that the container can be designed so that it can appeal to consumers. An important design goal is to make the container as user friendly as possible. The container should be convenient to be used by anyone. For example, when companies began to use plastic containers for condiment like ketchup, mustard, and mayonnaise, it became a great convenience for its users. In the beginning, condiments were stored in glass containers with lids that had to be screwed off. Then the user had to pour the ketchup or mustard on the food, which became a messy task, or scoop it out with a spoon. However, flexible plastic containers were much easier to use. All you had to do was hold the container over the food, and squeeze it until the condiment came out. It was much faster and easier than having to remove a lid and pour it out. Another important design is to give the container a pleasing appearance, so that buyers can display it in their homes. For example, a cookie company can sell their cookies not inside a plain cardboard box, but rather in a nice metal box. The company can decorate the metal box with nice pictures so that when consumers present the cookies to their guests, the cookies will look nice and classy. Attractive containers can make the product more appealing to purchase for the consumers.	비즈니스 클래스의 강의를 들으시오. 소비자들이 상품을 구매하기 위해 상점에 들어서면, 그들은 단지 상품 자체를 구매하는 것이 아니에요. 그들은 또한 물건이 담기는 용기를 구입합니다. 그래서 용기의 디자인이 중요해요. 구매자가 어떤 브랜드를 살 것인지 결정할 때 그것이 결정적인 요소가 될 수 있어서 매우 중요하죠. 오늘 우리는 용기가 소비자들에게 어필할 수 있도록 설계될 수 있는 몇 가지 방법에 대해 논의할 겁니다. 중요한 설계 목표는 용기를 가능한 한 사용자 친화적으로 만드는 것입니다. 용기는 누구나 사용할 수 있도록 편리해야 하죠. 예를 들어, 회사들이 케첩, 겨자, 마요네즈 같은 조미료에 플라스틱 용기를 사용하기 시작했을 때, 그것은 사용자들에게 큰 편리함이 되었습니다. 초기에는 조미료를 뚜껑이 달린 유리 용기에 보관했어요. 그리고 나서 사용자는 음식에 케첩이나 겨자를 부어야 했고, 그것은 지저분해지거나 또는 숟가락으로 퍼내야 했어요. 그러나 말랑말랑한 플라스틱 용기는 훨씬 사용하기 쉬웠죠. 용기에 음식을 담아서 조미료가 나올 때까지 짜기만 하면 되니까요. 뚜껑을 열고 붓는 것보다 훨씬 빠르고 쉽죠. 또 다른 중요한 디자인은 용기를 보기 좋게 만들어 구매자들이 집에 진열할 수 있도록 하는 것입니다. 예를 들어, 쿠키 회사는 그들의 쿠키를 평범한 종이 상자에 담아 파는 것이 아니라, 멋진 금속 상자에 담아 팔 수 있어요. 이 회사는 소비자들이 손님들에게 쿠키를 선물할 때 쿠키가 멋지고 고급스러워 보이도록 금속 상자를 멋진 그림으로 장식합니다. 매력적인 용기는 그 제품이 소비자들에게 더 매력적으로 보이게 할 수 있어요.

예시 답변

이 교수는 강연에서 제품의 용기가 소비자에게 어필할 수 있도록 설계할 수 있는 두 가지 방법을 설명한다. 한 가지 설계 목표는 용기를 가능한 한 사용자 친화적으로 만드는 것이다. 예를 들어, 회사들은 케첩, 겨자, 마요네즈와 같은 조미료에 플라스틱 용기를 사용하기 시작했다. 과거에 그것들은 유리 용기에 보관되어 있어 뚜껑을 열어야만 했다. 그러면 케첩이나 겨자를 음식에 부어야 하는데, 그것은 지저분할 것이다. 그러나 플라스틱 용기는 쉽게 사용할 수 있어서 사용하기에 더 매력적이었다. 뚜껑을 여는 것보다 훨씬 빠르고 쉬웠다.

용기를 보기 좋은 모습으로 만들어 소비자들이 집에서 마음 편히 진열할 수 있도록 하는 것도 디자인 목표다. 예를 들어, 쿠키를 파는 회사는 종이 상자 대신 멋진 금속 상자에 쿠키를 팔 수도 있다. 금속 상자는 소비자들이 손님에게 상자를 선물할 때 멋지고 매력적으로 보일 수 있도록 멋진 그림으로 장식될 것이다. 이것은 그 제품을 더욱 매력적으로 만들 것이다. 따라서, 이것이 제품의 용기가 소비자들에게 어필하도록 설계되는 두 가지 방법이다.

Page.115

연습5

Question 4 of 4

강의의 예시를 들어, 고대 로마 도시들이 확장될 수 있었던 두 가지 발전 요인에 대해 설명하라.

Listen to a lecture in a history class.

Cities from the ancient world tend to be small, usually restricted to sources of water, like rivers. The ancient cities could not expand since they could not cross the rivers, or be far from their important water sources. However, ancient Roman cities grew larger compared to the other ancient cities. They were able to do this because of their advanced technology.

One advanced technology which allowed the Roman cities to expand was their advanced building material. Ancient Romans had developed a special concrete that would harden even under water. This water resistant concrete made building new structures possible. For instance, the Romans used these concrete to build improved bridges that were able to cross wide rivers and also transport materials using wagons and carts. Due to these strong bridges, Roman cities were able to be built on both sides of the water, resulting in large cities that would have been impossible without the special building material.

Another technology that helped the Romans expand their cities was the development of a system that delivered fresh, clean water. This system was called aqueduct, and it brought the water the Romans needed. Aqueducts are a series of open channels that stretch from the source, high in the mountains, to cities below. Aqueducts were carefully planned and developed so that even a minor drop in altitude would provide a constant flow of water to the cities. The aqueducts allowed enormous amounts of water to be transported over long distances. It even brought fresh water to places far from rivers. With aqueducts, people were able to have water to drink and bathe without being near a river. So ancient Roman cities were able to grow in new locations.

역사 수업의 강의를 들으시오.

고대 도시들은 작은 경향이 있고, 보통 강과 같은 수원에 의해 제한됩니다. 고대 도시들은 강을 건너지 못했기 때문에, 혹은 그들의 중요한 수원에서 멀리 떨어져 있기 때문에 확장될 수 없었지요. 그러나 고대 로마의 도시들은 다른 고대 도시들에 비해 규모가 컸습니다. 그것은 진보된 기술 덕분에 가능했어요.

로마 도시들이 확장될 수 있게 해준 한 가지 진보된 기술은 그들의 발전된 건축 재료였습니다. 고대 로마인들은 물속에서도 굳을 수 있는 특별한 콘크리트를 개발했습니다. 이 내수 콘크리트는 새로운 구조물을 지을 수 있게 했어요. 예를 들어, 로마인들은 넓은 강을 건널 수 있는 개선된 다리를 건설하기 위해 이 콘크리트를 사용했고 마차나 카트를 이용하여 재료들을 운반하기도 했습니다. 이러한 튼튼한 다리 덕분에 로마의 도시들은 물 양쪽에 건설될 수 있었고, 그 결과 특별한 건축 재료가 없었다면 불가능했을 대도시들이 생겨났습니다.

로마인들이 그들의 도시를 확장하는 데 도움을 준 또 다른 기술은 신선하고 깨끗한 물을 공급하는 시스템의 개발이었습니다. 이 체계는 수로라고 불렸고, 로마인들이 필요로 하는 물을 가져왔습니다. 수로는 높은 산지에서 아래 도시로 이어지는 일련의 개방된 통로입니다. 수로는 고도가 조금만 떨어져도 도시로 물이 끊임없이 흐르도록 세심하게 계획되고 개발되었어요. 수로는 엄청난 양의 물이 먼 거리를 통과하도록 했죠. 그것은 심지어 강에서 멀리 떨어진 곳에 신선한 물을 가져다 주기도 했습니다. 수로가 있어서 사람들은 강 근처에 있지 않고도 마시고 목욕할 수 있는 물을 얻을 수 있었습니다. 그래서 고대 로마의 도시들은 새로운 장소에서 성장할 수 있었습니다.

예시 답변

교수는 이 강연에서 고대 로마 도시들이 확장될 수 있었던 두 가지 발전에 대해 설명한다. 우선, 로마인들은 더 진보된 기술을 가지고 있었고 그래서 로마인들은 진보된 건축 자재를 가지고 있었다. 그들은 물 속에서 굳는 특별한 콘크리트를 가지고 있었다. 이것은 새로운 종류의 구조물을 짓는 것을 가능하게 했다. 이 특별한 콘크리트 덕분에, 로마인들은 더 좋은 다리를 만들 수 있었다. 다리로 넓은 강을 건널 수 있었고 마차와 수레로 자재를 수송할 수 있었다. 그래서 이 다리들로 로마 도시들은 강의 양쪽에 건설될 수 있었다.

게다가, 고대 로마인들은 깨끗한 물을 운반하는 방법을 개발했다. 로마인들은 사람들에게 물을 운반하기 위해 수도관을 지었다. 수로는 산에서 도시로 물을 수송하는 일련의 개방된 통로다. 그것은 고도가 떨어지면서 도시로 지속적으로 물을 공급할 수 있도록 세심하게 계획되고 건설되었다. 수로들은 많은 양의 물을 아주 먼 거리로 이동시켰고 강에서 멀리 떨어진 곳으로 신선한 물을 가져왔다. 그래서 사람들은 강 옆에 있지 않아도 마시고 목욕할 수 있는 깨끗한 물을 얻었다. 그리고 도시들은 새로운 장소에서 성장할 수 있었다.

Actual Test 01

Page.123

Question 1 of 4

학교에서 학생들은 다양한 학업 과제를 완성해야 한다. 아래 과제 중 어떤 것이 학생들에게 유익하다고 생각하는가?
   1) 연구 논문
   2) 수업 발표
   3) 그룹 프로젝트
응답에 구체적 예제와 세부 사항을 포함시키시오

notes:

Question 2 of 4

음악관 오픈 시간

학생들이 악기 연주를 할 연습실을 예약할 수 있는 캠퍼스 음악관은 매일 밤 9시에 문을 닫는다. 하지만, 나는 학교가 자정까지는 음악관을 개방해야 한다고 생각한다. 악기를 소지한 학생들은 늦은 밤에 연습하고 싶어 하는 경우가 많지만 이들을 수용할 수 있는 시설이 없다. 또한 많은 학생들이 연습실을 이용하고 싶어하지만, 제한된 방 개수 때문에 예약하기가 어렵다. 음악관 운영 시간이 길어진다면 학생들이 연습실을 예약하기가 더 쉬울 것이다.

Now listen to two students discussing the letter.

W: Hey, did you see the letter in the newspaper today?

M: Sure did. I'm glad the school is finally extending the hours.

W: It would be so wonderful for us music students to have somewhere with longer hours to practice in. I mean right now, students practice in their dorm rooms since the music building closes so early.

M: Actually, I do that a lot. I play my cello in my dorm room.

W: Me too! I always felt sorry to my neighbors because even if I tried to keep the volume down, it's still pretty loud. The other students in the dorm are probably sleeping or studying.

M: That's true.

W: Also, we could really use some extra time slots. During the big concert season, like winter and spring, everyone in the orchestra need to practice their parts.

M: I know! Every time I try to practice during the concert season, I fail to get a room because everyone is standing in line to practice.

W: So extending the hours of the music building will really benefit the students.

이제 두 학생이 편지에 대해 토론하는 것을 들으시오.

W: 야, 너 오늘 신문에 난 편지 봤어?

M: 당연하지. 드디어 학교가 시간을 연장했다니 기뻐.

W: 우리 음대 학생들이 더 오래 연습할 곳이 생겼다니 정말 멋진 일이야. 내 말은, 지금은 음악관이 너무 일찍 닫는 바람에 학생들이 기숙사 방에서 연습하고 있다는 거야.

M: 사실, 나도 자주 그러고 있어. 나도 내 기숙사 방에서 첼로를 연주해.

W: 나도! 음량을 낮추려고 노력하지만 여전히 꽤 시끄러워서 이웃들에게 늘 미안한 마음이야. 기숙사에 있는 다른 학생들은 아마 잠을 자거나 공부를 하고 있을 거야.

M: 맞아.

W: 또한, 우리는 남는 시간을 활용할 수도 있을 거야. 겨울과 봄처럼 큰 규모의 콘서트 시즌에는 오케스트라 구성원 모두가 자기 파트를 연습해야 돼.

M: 맞아! 콘서트 시즌 동안은 연습하려고 할 때마다 모두가 연습을 위해 줄을 서기 때문에 방을 잡을 수가 없어.

W: 그래서 음악관의 시간 연장은 학생들에게 큰 도움이 될 거야.

여자는 편집자에게 보내는 학생의 편지에 대해 자신의 의견을 제시한다. 그녀의 의견과 그 의견을 지지하는 이유를 설명하시오

Page.126

Question 3 of 4

반박하고 설득하라

종종, 기업들은 소비자들이 그들의 제품이나 서비스에 대한 부정적인 인상이 강해졌을 것이라는 사실을 알아차린다. 이를 해결하기 위해 기업들은 반박과 설득으로 알려진 광고 기법을 사용한다. 이 기법은 제품의 단점을 나타내는 광고를 포함하지만, 제품을 구매하여 사용할 때의 장점과 함께 제품이 가지고 있을 수 있는 문제점을 보완하는 방법을 보여 주어 그 단점을 반박하거나 그 단점에 도전한다. 이 방법을 사용하면, 기업들은 단점에도 불구하고 그 제품이나 서비스를 구매하도록 소비자들을 설득할 수 있다.

Now listen to a lecture in a business class. Let me give you an example of this topic. The other day, I was watching the television and an advertisement for a well-known pots and pans company showed up. In the television ad, a professional female chef appears before the screen and tells the viewers that she uses the company's pots and pans in her own kitchen. The chef begins the advertisement by mentioning the fact that the company's pots and pans are expensive. She admits to the viewers that the cost is more expensive compared to other brands. The chef agrees that when consumers go shopping for pots and pans, they might not want to spend so much money on the kitchenware since there are other pots and pans at the store which will cost far less. However, she goes on to explain that the higher cost is actually worth it because even though the pots and pans are expensive to purchase in the beginning, they actually save the consumer money in the long term. This is because these pots and pans come with a special lifetime warranty, which means that the company would replace the pots and pans if anything were to go wrong. This lifetime warranty is actually something that other companies cannot say about their products.	이제 경영학 클래스의 강의를 들으시오. 이 주제에 대한 예를 들어보겠습니다. 며칠 전에 텔레비전을 보고 있는데 유명한 취사도구 회사의 광고가 나왔습니다. 텔레비전 광고에서 전문 여성 요리사가 화면 앞에 나타나 시청자들에게 자기 집 주방에서 그 회사의 취사도구를 사용한다고 말했죠. 요리사는 그 회사의 취사도구가 비싸다는 사실을 언급하면서 광고를 시작했습니다. 그녀는 시청자들에게 다른 브랜드에 비해 가격이 비싸다는 것을 인정했습니다. 요리사는 소비자들이 취사도구를 사러 갈 때, 그 가게에 훨씬 가격이 저렴한 다른 취사도구들이 있기 때문에 부엌 용기에 그렇게 많은 돈을 쓰고 싶지 않을 수도 있다는 것에 동의했어요. 그러나 그녀는 취사도구를 구입하는 데 초기 비용이 많이 들긴 하지만, 장기적으로는 사실상 소비 비용을 절약하는 것이기 때문에 실제로는 더 높은 비용을 지불할 가치가 있다고 설명했습니다. 이 취사도구들에는 특별한 평생 보증서가 붙어있기 때문인데, 이는 만약 잘못된 일이 생기면 회사가 취사도구들을 교체해 주겠다는 것을 의미합니다. 이 평생 보증이야말로 사실 다른 회사들이 그들의 제품에 대해 말할 때 언급할 수 없는 것이죠.

강의의 예시를 들어, 그것이 반박하고 설득하기라는 개념과 어떤 관련이 있는지 설명하라.

Question 4 of 4

강의의 요점과 예시를 이용하여 호수가 자연에서 사라질 수 있는 두 가지 요인을 설명하시오.

Now listen to a lecture in a business class.
We assume that lakes are bodies of water that are permanent, something that will last forever. Actually, lakes are not permanent since they can actually disappear. Some lakes disappear from natural processes, while others disappear from the actions of human activities.

One way lakes can disappear naturally is by getting filled in with organic sediment. This process can often be seen in lakes with lots of plants growing in them. When these plants in the lakes die, they fall to the bottom of the lake and start to decompose. They are replaced by new plants that also eventually die and fall to the bottom of the lake. After many years, the dead plant matter build up at the bottom of the lake. When the dead plant matter build up, there is less and less space for water and eventually, the lake becomes completely full of dead plant matter. Thus, lakes disappear from the filling of dead plants.

Another way lakes can disappear is through human activities, and sometimes the lakes may disappear at a rapid rate. Farmers need water to irrigate their crops. They may use water from a nearby lake to farm. They will install pipes that connect the lake to their farm, so that lake water will be pumped out of the lake to water their crops. This irrigation system will be ok as long as the lake is refilled with rainwater or from streams that connect to the lake. But if there is no external source of water to replace the water that farmers use from the lake, the lake will eventually dry up.

지질학 수업의 강의를 들으시오.
우리는 호수가 영원히 존재할, 영구적인 수원이라고 추측합니다. 사실, 호수는 실제로 사라질 수 있기 때문에 영구적이지 않습니다. 어떤 호수는 자연적인 과정에서 사라지는 반면, 다른 호수는 인간의 활동으로 사라집니다.

호수가 자연적으로 사라질 수 있는 한 가지 경우는 유기적 퇴적물로 채워지는 것입니다. 이 과정은 종종 많은 식물들이 자라는 호수에서 볼 수 있습니다. 호수에 있는 식물들이 죽으면 호수 바닥으로 떨어져 부패하기 시작하죠. 그것들은 새로운 식물로 대체되는데, 이 식물 또한 결국 죽어서 호수 바닥으로 떨어집니다. 여러 해가 지나면 죽은 식물이 호수 바닥에 쌓입니다. 죽은 식물이 쌓이면 물이 있을 공간이 점점 줄어들고 결국 호수는 완전히 죽은 식물로 가득 차게 됩니다. 따라서, 호수는 죽은 식물이 가득하게 되어 사라지게 되죠.

호수가 사라질 수 있는 또 다른 경우는 인간의 활동에 의한 것이며, 때때로 호수는 빠른 속도로 사라질 수도 있습니다. 농부들은 농작물에 댈 물이 필요합니다. 그들은 농사를 짓기 위해 근처 호수의 물을 사용할 수도 있습니다. 그들은 호수와 그들의 농장을 연결하는 파이프를 설치하여 호수 물을 퍼내어 농작물에 물을 줄 겁니다. 이 관개 시스템은 호수가 빗물로 다시 채워지거나 시냇물과 연결되어 있는 한 괜찮습니다. 그러나 만약 농부들이 호수로부터 사용하는 물을 대체할 외부 수원이 없다면, 호수는 결국 말라버릴 겁니다.

Actual Test 02

Page.135

Question 1 of 4
어떤 사람들은 주변에 다른 사람들이 있는 공공 장소에서 공부하는 것을 선호한다. 다른 사람들은 주변에 사람이 거의 없거나 아예 없는 사적인 장소에서 공부하는 것을 선호한다. 당신은 어느 곳을 더 선호하는가?

notes:

Question 2 of 4

자전거 보관함에서 낡은 자전거 제거

나는 어떤 캠퍼스 자전거 보관함이든 그 옆을 지날 때마다 자물쇠로 잠겨 오랫동안 이동하지 않은 자전거들이 있다는 것을 알게 됐다. 대학은 이 자전거들을 보관함에서 치워 버려야 한다. 첫째, 자전거 소유주들이 자전거에 대해 잊어버렸기 때문에 자전거가 없어졌다는 것을 눈치채지 못할 것이다. 하지만 더 중요한 것은, 이 자전거들을 버리는 것이 보관함의 공간을 확보하는데 도움이 될 것이고, 그래서 실제로 자전거를 사용하는 사람들이 자전거를 주차할 수 있는 장소를 확보할 수 있을 것이다.

Now listen to two students discussing the letter.

W: I completely agree with the writer regarding the unused bicycles.

M: Hmm.. I agree that the university should throw the bikes away, but it might not be fair.

W: Not fair? Assuming that no one wants them? I think it would be a safe assumption that no one wants the bikes, based on the conditions they are in. Some of these bikes are missing parts, like handle bars and wheels. Others are rusty, as if they were left out for many years.

M: The bikes with the missing parts do look like they have not been used for a long time. But what if some are being used by students?

W: Well just to be safe, the school can attach notes on the bikes and give the owners two weeks to remove them, or they would be forcefully removed by campus security.

M: I guess that could work.

W: Plus, it would be a great advantage if they were gone.

M: Oh, I agree.

W: For example, in front of the dining hall, there are so many unused bikes so it's hard to find an empty space to park your bike.

M: Yes, it is pretty bad. Many students ride their bikes these days too.

W: The university also prohibits students from tying their bikes to posts or fences. So I have to always park my bike in a different building and walk over to the dining hall since there is hardly any space there.

이제 두 학생이 편지에 대해 토론하는 것을 들으시오.

W: 사용하지 않는 자전거에 대해서 필자의 의견에 전적으로 동의해.

M: 음.. 나는 대학이 자전거를 버려야 한다는 것에 동의하지만, 그것은 공정하지 않을 수도 있어.

W: 공정하지 않아? 아무도 그것을 원하지 않는다면? 나는 자전거들이 처한 상태로 볼 때 아무도 그것을 원하지 않는다고 생각해. 이 자전거들 중 몇몇은 핸들 바나 바퀴와 같은 부품들이 빠져 있어. 다른 것들은 몇 년 간 방치된 것처럼 녹슬어 있고.

M: 부품이 빠진 자전거는 오랫동안 사용하지 않은 것 같아. 하지만 몇 개는 학생들이 사용하고 있다면 어떨까?

W: 음, 만약을 위해서, 학교는 자전거에 메모를 부착하고, 소유주들에게 2주 동안 그것들을 치우도록 할 수 있어. 그렇지 않으면, 학교 경비에 의해 강제로 철거될 거야.

M: 그게 효과가 있을 것 같아.

W: 게다가, 방치된 자전거들이 사라진다면 큰 이점이 있을 거야.

M: 오, 나도 동의해.

W: 예를 들어, 식당 앞에는 사용하지 않는 자전거가 너무 많아서 자전거를 주차할 빈 공간을 찾기가 힘들어.

M: 맞아, 별로 좋지 않아. 요즘 많은 학생들이 자전거를 타니까.

W: 또한 대학은 학생들이 자전거를 기둥이나 울타리에 묶는 것을 금지하고 있어. 그래서 나는 항상 내 자전거를 다른 건물에 주차하고 식당으로 걸어가야 해. 왜냐하면 그곳에는 공간이 거의 없기 때문이야.

여자는 편집자에게 보내는 학생의 편지에 대해 의견을 말한다. 그녀의 의견과 그 의견을 주장하는 이유를 설명하시오.

Question 3 of 4

분산 저장

특정 환경에서, 식량은 일년 중 일정 기간 동안은 풍부하고 다른 기간 동안은 부족하다. 많은 동물들이 이런 환경에서 산다. 여기서, 동물들은 식량이 풍부하면 몇 달 동안 식량을 수집하고 준비할 것이고, 나중에 찾을 수 있는 식량이 적어질 때를 위해 저장해 둘 것이다. 이 수집 동물들은 분산 저장을 할 수 있다. 분산 수집 동물들은 다른 수집 동물들과 다르게, 그들의 식량을 한 곳에 보관하지 않는다. 그들은 식량을 여러 곳에 나누어 숨겨서 분산시킬 것이다. 식량이 부족할 때, 수집 동물들은 이러한 은신처에서 그들의 식량을 되찾을 것이다

Now listen to part of a lecture in a biology class. Alright class. So we actually see these kinds of animals live in parts of the world that become very cold in winter. For instance, in the northeastern area of the United States, a species of squirrel performs scatter hoarding. Like most squirrels, these species also enjoy eating nuts, since it is their primary source of food. During the cold winter months, nuts are very difficult to find. But during fall, the nuts can be found everywhere, since they fall from the tree during that season. So during the fall, the squirrels will spend time looking for nuts and once they find it, they will spend additional time preparing it. The preparation process involves the squirrel taking off the outer shell and cleaning the nut inside. This actually helps preserve the nut and will make it easier to eat the nut later. After the preparation, the squirrel will dig a hole and bury the nut. In a single season, the squirrel may bury hundreds of nuts. However, the nuts will not be stored in a big hole dug by the animal. The squirrel will have dug hundreds of little holes and stored each nut in their individual holes. The squirrel does this because even if another animal happens to find a nut buried in the ground, there will be many other nuts buried around, enough for the squirrel to eat and survive the winter.	이제 생물 수업에서 강의의 일부를 들어보자. 좋아요 여러분. 그래서 우리는 실제로 이런 종류의 동물들이 겨울에 매우 추워지는 일부 지역에 살고 있는 것을 볼 수 있습니다. 예를 들어, 미국의 북동부 지역에서는 다람쥐의 한 종이 분산 저장을 합니다. 대부분의 다람쥐들처럼, 이 종들도 견과류를 먹는 것을 즐깁니다. 왜냐하면 견과류는 그들의 주요 식량이기 때문입니다. 추운 겨울 동안에는 견과류를 찾기가 매우 어렵습니다. 하지만 가을 동안 견과류는 나무에서 떨어지기 때문에 어디에서나 찾을 수 있습니다. 그래서 가을 동안, 다람쥐들은 견과류를 찾는데 시간을 보낼 것이고, 일단 견과류를 찾으면, 그들은 견과류를 준비하는 데 추가로 시간을 보낼 것입니다. 준비 과정은 다람쥐가 겉껍질을 벗기고 안에 있는 견과를 깨끗이 하는 과정입니다. 이것은 실제로 견과류를 보존하는데 도움을 주고 나중에 견과류를 먹기 쉽게 만들 것입니다. 준비를 마친 다람쥐는 구멍을 파고 견과류를 묻을 것입니다. 한 계절에, 다람쥐는 수백 개의 견과류를 묻을지도 모릅니다. 하지만 견과류는 동물이 파 놓은 하나의 큰 구멍에 저장되지 않을 것입니다. 이 다람쥐는 수백 개의 작은 구멍을 파서 견과류를 각각의 구멍에 보관할 것입니다. 다람쥐가 이렇게 하는 것은 다른 동물이 우연히 땅속에 묻혀 있는 견과류를 발견하더라도, 다람쥐가 겨울을 날 수 있을 만큼의 다른 견과류가 주변에 많이 묻혀 있을 것이기 때문입니다.

강의의 예시를 들어, 그것이 어떻게 분산 저장 개념과 관련이 있는지 설명하시오.

Question 4 of 4

강의의 요점과 예시를 이용하여 기업이 다양성을 가질 수 있는 두 가지 방법을 설명하시오.

Listen to a lecture in a business class.

It's a given fact that businesses want to sell their products as much as possible. Most of the time, a business will sell one type of product, however the product may decrease in sales later because potential customers may have already purchased it. In such situations, companies will try to diversify, where companies will develop new or diverse products so that their sales will increase again. There are a few efficient methods companies can use to diversify their existing resources.

One method companies use to diversify is to use an existing technology to make a new product. Since the company already has the machines and technology to make a certain product, at times, the company can use the same machine and technology to make a different product. For instance, a company that makes televisions may start to make computer monitors since the technology that is used to make these two electronics are similar. So the company can use its existing machine and technology to make the computer monitors. The computer monitors will reach new customers who have no need for television screens, such as businesses that need to buy computer monitors for their workers.

Another method companies use to diversify is by appealing to its existing customers with a new product. The existing customers are one of the most important assets of any company, and these customers may have other needs that the company can cater to with an alternative product. For example, a ski company may have a large group of customers who enjoy winter sports. So the company might start making ski jackets, since the customers who buy the ski from them will also need warm ski jackets. Since the customers like the company's skis, they are likely to buy the jackets with the company's name on it.

경영학 수업을 들어보자.

기업들이 제품을 가능한 한 많이 팔기를 원하는 것은 당연한 사실입니다. 대부분의 경우, 기업은 한 종류의 제품을 판매할 것이지만, 잠재 고객이 이미 구매했을 수 있기 때문에 그 제품은 나중에 판매가 감소할 수 있습니다. 이런 상황에서 기업들은 새로운 제품이나 다양한 제품을 개발하여 매출이 다시 증가하도록 하는 다변화를 시도할 겁니다. 기업들이 기존의 자원을 다양화하기 위해 사용할 수 있는 몇 가지 효율적인 방법이 있습니다.

기업들이 다각화를 위해 사용하는 한 가지 방법은 새로운 제품을 만들기 위해 기존의 기술을 사용하는 것입니다. 이미 특정 제품을 만드는 기계와 기술을 보유하고 있기 때문에 같은 기계와 기술을 사용하여 다른 제품을 만들 수 있는 경우도 있죠. 예를 들어, 텔레비전을 만드는 회사는 컴퓨터 모니터를 만들기 시작할 것인데, 이 두 전자 제품을 만드는 데 사용되는 기술이 비슷하기 때문입니다. 그래서 그 회사는 기존의 기계와 기술을 사용하여 컴퓨터 모니터를 만들 수 있습니다. 컴퓨터 모니터는 직원들을 위해 컴퓨터 모니터를 사야 하는 사업체 등과 같이 텔레비전이 필요 없는 새로운 고객들에게 다가갈 겁니다.

기업이 다양화를 위해 사용하는 또 다른 방법은 기존 고객에게 신제품으로 어필하는 것입니다. 기존 고객들은 어느 기업에서나 가장 중요한 자산 중 하나이며, 이러한 고객들은 회사가 대체 상품으로 충족시켜줄 수 있는 또 다른 필요를 가지고 있을 수 있어요. 예를 들어, 스키 회사는 겨울 스포츠를 즐기는 큰 고객 집단을 가질 수 있죠. 그래서 그 회사는 스키 재킷을 만들기 시작할지도 모릅니다. 왜냐하면 그들에게 스키를 사는 고객들은 따뜻한 스키 재킷도 필요로 할 것이기 때문입니다. 고객들은 그 회사의 스키를 좋아하기 때문에 회사 이름이 적힌 재킷을 살 가능성이 높습니다.

Actual Test 03

Page.147

Question 1 of 4
당신은 다음 진술에 동의하십니까, 동의하지 않으십니까? 아이들이 직업을 선택할 때 부모의 참여가 필요하다. 답변에 구체적인 예시와 세부 사항을 포함시키십시오.

notes:

Question 2 of 4

캠퍼스 공사

보도, 주차장 정비 등 학교 내 소규모 공사가 학생들의 수업이 있는 정규 학기 중에 종종 일어납니다. 나는 가능하다면 학교가 여름 방학 동안 공사 프로젝트를 진행 해야 한다고 제안합니다. 첫째, 이러한 공사 프로젝트는 여러 면에서 상당한 지장을 줄 수 있습니다. 그것들은 불편함을 야기시키고 학생들이 캠퍼스를 돌아다니는 것을 어렵게 할 수 있습니다. 또한, 공사 프로젝트가 여름에 계획되었다면 일반적으로 날씨가 좋기 때문에 더 빨리 끝날 것입니다.

M: So what do you think of the letter's proposal?
W: I think it will be a great idea!
M: So you agree with the problems that occurred from the constructions?
W: Yes, I do. For example, I know you don't drive to school, but I do. And every day I drive to school, I need to find a place to park my car. Remember last year, when the university decided to repair the parking lots?
M: Yes, I remember. There was a lot of construction going on. I think it started in December.
W: Yup. At least four of the parking lots were closed. Which meant that there was not enough parking spots for students and professors. I had to circle around, looking for a parking space, and when I did manage to find one in the streets, I had to walk all the way to the classroom.
M: Yikes, that must have been annoying.
W: It was. It actually happened to a lot of other students in my class. My classmates always arrived late having trouble finding a parking spot. Sometimes, my professors were late as well.
M: Oh no…
W: Also, the letter's second point makes sense. For instance, one of the reasons why the repairs on the parking lots lasted for a long time last year was because of the snow storms. The construction workers had to keep stopping, sometimes for weeks because of the snow and ice on the ground.
M: I actually remember that! We had several snowstorms back to back last year.
W: So with all the pauses in between the work because of the weather, the construction took longer than expected.

M: 그래, 그 편지의 제안에 대해 어떻게 생각해?
W: 좋은 생각이라 생각해!
M: 그럼 공사 때문에 생긴 문제들에 동의하는 거야?
W: 응. 예를 들어, 네가 운전해서 학교에 가지 않는 건 알지만, 난 그렇지 않아. 매일 차를 몰고 학교에 가는데, 차를 주차할 장소를 찾아야 해. 작년에 대학교에서 주차장을 수리하기로 결정했을 때 기억나?
M: 응, 기억나. 수많은 공사들이 한창이었지. 12월에 시작한 것 같아.
W: 응. 적어도 4개의 주차장이 문을 닫았어. 그것은 학생들과 교수들을 위한 충분한 주차 공간이 없다는 것을 의미해. 나는 주차 공간을 찾으면서 주위를 빙글빙글 돌아야 했고, 거리에서 주차 할 곳을 찾으면, 나는 교실까지 걸어가야 했어.
M: 아이쿠, 정말 짜증 났겠다.
W: 응. 실제로 우리 반의 많은 다른 학생들에게도 그런 일이 있었어. 우리 반 친구들은 주차할 곳을 찾기 어려워서 항상 늦게 도착했어. 가끔은 우리 교수님들도 늦으셨어.
M: 이런…
W: 또한, 그 편지의 두 번째 요점은 말이 돼. 예를 들어, 작년에 주차장 수리가 오랫동안 지속된 이유 중 하나는 눈보라 때문이었어. 건설 노동자들은 종종 땅 위의 눈과 얼음 때문에 몇 주 동안 공사를 계속 멈춰야 했지.
M: 기억이 나! 작년에는 눈보라가 몇 차례 있었어.
W: 날씨 때문에 공사가 중간 중간 멈춰서 공사하는 데 예상보다 시간이 오래 걸렸어.

여자는 편집자에게 보내는 학생의 편지에 대해 의견을 말한다. 그녀의 의견과 그녀가 그 의견을 지지하는 이유를 설명하시오.

Page.150

Question 3 of 4

정서 지능

인간의 지능은 복잡한 생각을 분석하고 이해하는 정신적 능력으로 여겨진다. 많은 심리학자들은 다른 종류의 지능이 있다고 믿고 있는데, 이것을 정서 지능이라고 한다. 정서 지능을 가진 사람들은 자신의 진심을 인식하고 무엇이 그들의 감정을 일으키는지를 이해하는 능력을 가지고 있다. 정서 지능을 가진 사람들은 필요할 때, 그들의 감정을 바꾸거나 고치거나, 더 잘 조절할 수 있다. 이런 종류의 지능은 사람들이 사회적 환경에서 적절하게 행동하도록 도와주고, 그들이 다른 사람들과 좋은 관계를 유지하도록 도와준다.

Now listen to a lecture in a psychology class.
Here is an example of my daughter. Recently, my daughter invited her friend over to watch a movie. However, they got into an argument because they could not agree on which movie to watch. My daughter got really upset during the argument, which was not like her at all. Suddenly, my daughter stopped arguing and thought about why she was so upset. She realized that her reaction was uncalled for, and also that she was not actually upset with her friend. Something else had been bothering her. My daughter had just gotten a job as a summer camp counselor for kids. She was worried and stressed about her new job since she had never worked with children before. So my daughter came to an understanding that she was not upset about which movie to watch, but she was troubled about starting a new job. She wanted the job to go well and for the kids to like her. When my daughter realized this, she stopped arguing with her friend and apologized to her. She told her friend that she was anxious of starting her new job and apologized for getting upset at her. Her friend encouraged her and said that she would do a great job. Afterwards, my daughter felt better and the two were able to relax and watch a movie.

이제 심리학 수업의 강의를 들으시오.
여기 내 딸을 예시로 들겠습니다. 최근에 내 딸이 친구를 초대해서 영화를 봤습니다. 하지만 어떤 영화를 봐야 할지 의견이 맞지 않아 말다툼을 벌였죠. 내 딸은 말다툼을 하는 동안 정말 화가 났는데, 그것은 전혀 그녀답지 않았어요. 갑자기 딸아이는 말다툼을 멈추고 왜 그렇게 화가 났는지 생각해 보았죠. 그녀는 자신의 반응이 부적절하다는 것을 깨달았고, 또한 실제로 친구에게 화가 나지 않았다는 것을 깨달았습니다. 다른 무언가가 그녀를 괴롭히고 있었죠. 내 딸은 아이들을 위한 여름 캠프 상담원으로 막 취직했습니다. 그녀는 이전에 아이들과 함께 일한 적이 없었기 때문에 새로운 직업에 대해 걱정하고 스트레스를 받았습니다. 그래서 내 딸은 어떤 영화를 봐야 할지에 대해 화가 난 것이 아니라, 새로운 일을 시작하는 것에 대해 힘들어 하고 있다는 것을 알아차렸습니다. 그녀는 그 일이 잘 풀리고 아이들이 그녀를 좋아하기를 원했습니다. 딸이 이 사실을 깨닫게 되자 친구와의 말다툼을 중단하고 사과했습니다. 그녀는 친구에게 새 직장을 시작하는 것이 불안하다고 말했고, 그녀에게 화를 낸 것에 대해 사과했죠. 그녀의 친구는 그녀를 격려했고 그녀가 아주 잘 할 것이라고 말했습니다. 이후 딸의 기분이 좋아졌고 두 사람은 마음을 놓고 영화를 볼 수 있었습니다.

강의에서 언급된 예시를 들어, 그것이 어떻게 정서 지능의 개념과 관련이 있는지 설명하시오.

Question 4 of 4

강의에서 나온 도마뱀의 예를 이용하여 지표면 아래 이동의 두 가지 장점을 설명하시오.

Listen to a lecture from a biology class.

When humans move around, we walk on the surface. Many animals walk on the earth's surface as well. Cats, dogs, horses, and so on all walk across the surface of the earth. However, there are animals that move around from place to place beneath the soil. This movement underground is called subsurface locomotion. This form of movement actually has several benefits.

One advantage of subsurface locomotion is that it minimizes an animal's exposure to extreme temperature from the surface. This benefit is actually very important for animals that live in extreme environments, where it could be dangerous to spend a large amount of time on the surface. For instance, in the Sahara Desert, there lives a lizard that is able to move via subsurface locomotion. It moves through the sand very quickly so there is no need for it to move on the surface. By not being above ground, the lizard is also hidden from the dangerously high temperatures.

Another advantage subsurface locomotion provides is that it helps animals capture their prey. The prey animals on the surface cannot see the predators approaching them from underground. The lizard in the Sahara Desert is also a good example of this. When an insect is walking on the surface, it produces small vibrations in the sand. The lizard will sense these small vibrations, and it will move very quickly underground so that it cannot be seen, towards the origin of the vibrations. After approaching the target, the lizard will pop its head above the ground and capture the insect by surprise.

생물학 수업을 들으시오.

인간은 돌아다닐 때, 지표면 위를 걷습니다. 많은 동물들도 지구 표면 위를 걷죠. 고양이, 개, 말, 등등 모든 것들이 지구의 표면을 가로질러 걷습니다. 하지만 흙 아래 이곳 저곳을 돌아다니는 동물들이 있어요. 지하에 있는 이 운동을 지표면 아래 이동이라고 합니다. 이런 형태의 운동은 실제로 여러 가지 이점을 가지고 있습니다.

지표면 아래 이동의 한 가지 장점은 지표면의 극한의 온도에 대한 동물의 노출을 최소화한다는 것입니다. 이러한 이점은 지표면에서 많은 시간을 보내는 것이 위험할 수 있는 극한 환경에 사는 동물들에게 실제로 매우 중요합니다. 예를 들어, 사하라 사막에는 지표면 아래 이동을 통해 움직일 수 있는 도마뱀이 살고 있습니다. 그것은 모래를 통해 매우 빠르게 이동하기 때문에 지표면에서 움직일 필요가 없습니다. 도마뱀은 땅 위에 있지 않기 때문에 위험할 정도로 높은 온도에서도 숨을 수 있어요.

지표면 아래 이동의 또 다른 장점은 동물들이 먹이를 잡도록 돕는다는 것입니다. 지표면에 있는 먹잇감들은 지하에서 접근하는 포식자들을 볼 수 없습니다. 사하라 사막의 도마뱀도 이것의 좋은 예시입니다. 곤충이 지표면 위를 걸을 때, 그것은 모래 속에서 작은 진동을 일으킵니다. 도마뱀은 이 작은 진동을 감지하고, 진동의 기원을 향해, 보이지 않도록 지하에서 매우 빠르게 움직일 겁니다. 도마뱀은 표적에 접근한 뒤 땅 위로 머리를 쳐들어 곤충을 기습적으로 포획하죠.

Actual Test 04

Page.159

Question 1 of 4
당신이 다음 진술에 동의하는지 동의하지 않는지 진술하시오. 답변을 지지하기 위해 구체적인 세부 정보를 사용하여 그 이유를 설명하시오. **학생들은 대학에 입학하기 전에 아르바이트를 경험해야 한다.**

notes:

Question 2 of 4

도서관 작업 공간

도서관이 지어질 때부터, 주 캠퍼스 도서관에는 여러 사람이 쓸 수 있는 대형 스터디 테이블이 제공됐다. 올 여름부터는 대형 테이블이 개인 스터디를 위한 칸막이 책상으로 전환될 것이고, 개개인은 사생활 보호를 위한 칸으로 둘러싸여 공부할 수 있게 된다. 이 새로운 책상은 학생들을 격리시키고 도서관 안의 소음을 없애 학생들이 집중할 수 있도록 하는데 도움을 줄 것이다. 또한, 칸막이 책상은 도서관이 더 많은 학생을 수용할 수 있게 해줄 것이다. 현재의 스터디 테이블은 각각 6명의 학생을 수용할 수 있으며, 바닥 공간을 너무 많이 차지한다. 반면 칸막이 책상은 공간 효율성이 극대화되도록 설계되어 도서관 안에 새로운 좌석 50석을 추가할 수 있게 할 것이다.

Now listen to two students discussing the announcement.

M: The school is making a huge mistake.

W: What do you mean?

M: Well, the school is trying to eliminate distractions, so that students can study better. However with the multiperson tables gone, students will not be able to meet together to discuss group projects.

W: You're right, and group projects are common in classes these days.

M: So instead of spending money on these new cubicle tables, the school should really be spending the money building conference rooms. This would also help reduce the noise in the library.

W: That sounds a lot better than working in isolation.

M: Exactly. And the other thing is about overcrowding. Sure, we have more students than last year, but do we really have a problem with overcrowding?

W: I don't think so. I mean, I'm always using the entire table for myself.

M: Right? I see empty tables all the time. It will be a waste of money to replace what we have since what we have now is efficient for the number of students attending the university.

이제 두 학생이 발표에 대해 토론하는 것을 들으시오.

M: 학교가 엄청난 실수를 하고 있어.

W: 무슨 뜻이야?

M: 음, 학교는 학생들이 공부를 더 잘 할 수 있도록 주의를 흐트러뜨리는 것을 없애려고 노력하고 있어. 하지만 대형 테이블이 사라지면, 학생들은 그룹 프로젝트를 논의하기 위해 같이 모일 수 없을 거야.

W: 네 말이 맞아, 요즘 수업에는 그룹 프로젝트가 흔해.

M: 그래서 이 새로운 칸막이 테이블에 돈을 쓰는 대신에, 학교는 회의실을 짓는 데 돈을 써야 해. 이것은 또한 도서관의 소음을 줄이는데 도움이 될 거야.

W: 그건 혼자 일하는 것보다 훨씬 나을 것 같아.

M: 맞아. 그리고 또 다른 하나는 과밀화에 대한 이야기야. 물론, 작년보다 학생이 더 많아지긴 했는데, 정말 과밀화 문제가 있는 거 같아?

W: 난 그렇게 생각하지 않아. 내 말은, 난 항상 테이블 전체를 나 혼자 사용하고 있어.

M: 맞지? 나는 항상 빈 테이블이 있는 것을 봐. 현재 우리가 쓰고 있는 테이블은 우리 대학에 다니는 학생 수 대비 충분하기 때문에 우리가 쓰는 테이블을 대체하는 것은 낭비야.

남자는 대학의 발표에 대해 자신의 의견을 말한다. 그의 의견과 그 의견을 지지하는 이유를 설명하시오.

Question 3 of 4

의식화

과학자들은 동물들 사이의 의사소통 행동이 의식화라고 불리는 과정을 통해 발전된다고 믿는다. 의식화는 특정 행동이 시간이 지남에 따라 변화할 때 일어나는데, 원래 실용적인 목적을 가지고 있던 어떤 행동이 특정 메시지를 전달하는 것으로 진화하는 것이다. 예를 들어, 특정한 움직임이나 신체적 특징이 다른 동물들이 이해할 수 있는 신호나 경고의 역할을 하도록 바뀔 수 있다. 일단 그 행동이 의식화되면, 그것은 의사소통의 형태가 된다. 그래서 어떤 동물이 이 행동에 가담하면 다른 동물들은 그 행위의 의미를 빠르게 해석하고 그에 따라 반응할 것이다.

Now listen to a lecture in a zoology class.
In order to understand this concept, let's take a look at an example we are all familiar with. What is something dogs do when they are threatened? Or when they want to guard themselves? They show their teeth. When we see dogs baring their teeth, we make sure to stay away from them. Now let's take a look at how this behavior came to be a recognized communication. Long ago, dogs would prepare to bite whatever that was threatening them. It would prepare by baring its teeth. But the reason behind this was quite simple; the dog did not want to bite its own lips while biting the other animal. Interestingly, other dogs and animals came to realize that this teeth baring behavior always appeared before the dog was going to bite. So the animals saw it as a signal to be careful and that they should stay away or risk getting bitten. This situation later was also realized by the dog baring its teeth. It realized that baring its teeth was protection itself. So what started as a way of protecting itself from biting, evolved into a communication device to warn others. The dog realized that there was no need to attack, but could achieve the same result by showing the possibility of an attack by showing its teeth.

이제 동물학 수업의 강의를 들으시오.
이 개념을 이해하기 위해, 우리 모두가 익숙한 예를 살펴봅시다. 개가 위협을 받을 때 혹은 스스로를 지키고 싶을 때 하는 행동은 무엇일까요? 그들은 이빨을 드러냅니다. 개가 이빨을 드러내고 있는 것을 볼 때, 우리는 반드시 그들로부터 떨어져 있어야 합니다. 이제 이러한 행동이 어떻게 공인된 의사소통이 되었는지 살펴봅시다. 오래 전에, 개들은 자신들을 위협하는 어떤 것이든 물 준비를 하곤 했습니다. 이빨을 드러내며 준비하는 것이죠. 그러나 그 이면의 이유는 꽤 간단합니다. 개는 다른 동물을 물면서 자기 입술을 깨물고 싶지 않았습니다. 흥미롭게도, 다른 개들과 동물들은 개가 물기 전에 이 이빨을 드러내는 행동이 항상 나타났다는 것을 깨닫게 되었습니다. 그래서 동물들은 그것을 조심하라는 신호로 보고 멀리 떨어져 있거나 물릴 위험에 처해있다는 것을 알았죠. 개가 이를 드러내는 이러한 상황은 이후에 밝혀졌습니다. 이를 드러내는 것이 보호 자체라는 것을 깨달은 것이죠. 그래서 자신을 물지 않도록 보호하는 방법으로 시작된 것이 다른 사람들에게 경고하기 위한 의사소통 장치로 진화했습니다. 개는 공격할 필요는 없지만 이빨을 드러내어 공격의 가능성을 보여줌으로써 동일한 결과를 얻을 수 있다는 것을 깨달은 것입니다.

강의에서 논의된 개들의 예시를 이용하여 그것이 의식화의 개념과 어떻게 관련되는지 설명하시오.

Question 4 of 4

강의의 핵심 내용과 예시를 이용하여 확산의 개념을 설명하시오

Listen to a lecture in a sociology class.

Let's discuss about a particular cultural process: diffusion. Since the beginning, different cultures have taken advantage of each other's innovations they came into contact with. Diffusion occurs when something cultural, such as a custom, food, or invention is spread from one culture to another. One cultural group may adopt a cultural item from another group. Cultural diffusion occurs in many different ways: military conquest, tourism, or something as basic as satellite television shows. For instance, people in the United States read the newspaper on a daily basis. Did you ever consider where the letters and characters from the newspaper came from? They were borrowed from a different culture long ago. Then the printing of the words, which was borrowed from Germany, was taken. Finally, paper, which the Chinese first invented, was borrowed as well. These innovations from all over the world were shared between cultures and over time, the newspaper was able to be developed here in the United States. So cultural diffusion can occur over long distances, and over a long period of time.

Sometimes diffusion is selective. It's not always easy. For example, people in the United States have accepted the Asian medicine of acupuncture, which is using needles to cure pain. Many Americans have discovered that acupuncture is effective. But few understand the philosophy that supports acupuncture. People tend to resist ideas that seem too foreign, which might be too different from their own beliefs and values. However, the aspect which is not considered too different are adopted or diffused into their culture. So acupuncture has been diffused into the American minds, but not the philosophy behind it.

사회학 수업의 강의를 들으시오.

특정 문화적 과정인 확산에 대해 토론해 봅시다. 시작부터 서로 다른 문화들은 그들이 접촉하고 있는 서로 다른 혁신들을 이용해 왔습니다. 확산은 관습, 음식, 발명 같은 어떤 문화적인 것이 한 문화에서 다른 문화로 전파될 때 일어납니다. 한 문화적 그룹은 또 다른 그룹으로부터 하나의 문화적 요소를 채택할 수 있습니다. 문화 확산은 군사 정복, 관광, 또는 위성 텔레비전 쇼와 같은 기본적인 것 등 서로 다른 다양한 방법으로 일어납니다.

예를 들어, 미국 사람들은 매일 신문을 읽습니다. 당신은 신문에 나온 글자들과 인물들이 어디서 왔는지 생각해 본 적 있나요? 그것들은 오래 전에 다른 문화권에서 차용된 것입니다. 그리고 나서 독일로부터 차용된 글자 인쇄술이 사용되었습니다. 마침내 중국인들이 처음 발명한 종이도 빌려왔죠. 전 세계의 이러한 혁신은 문화 사이에서 공유되었고 시간이 지나면서 미국에서 신문이 개발될 수 있었습니다. 그래서 문화 확산은 먼 거리, 그리고 오랜 시간에 걸쳐 일어날 수 있었습니다.

때때로 확산은 선택적입니다. 항상 쉬운 것은 아니에요. 예를 들어, 미국 사람들은 고통을 치료하기 위해 바늘을 사용하는, 침술이라는 아시아의 의술을 받아들였습니다. 많은 미국인들은 침술이 효과적이라는 것을 발견했어요. 그러나 침술을 지탱하고 있는 철학을 이해하는 사람은 거의 없습니다. 사람들은 자신의 신념과 가치관과 많이 다른, 너무 이국적으로 보이는 생각에 저항하는 경향이 있어요. 그러나 크게 다르지 않은 것들은 채택되거나 그들의 문화에 확산됩니다. 그래서 침술은 미국인의 마음에 확산되어 왔지만, 그 이면의 철학은 그러지 못했지요.

Actual Test 05

Page.171

Question 1 of 4
당신이 다음 진술에 동의하는지 동의하지 않는지 말하시오. 당신의 답변을 지지하기 위해 구체적인 세부 정보를 사용하여 이유를 설명하시오. 다른 문화에 대해 배우는 것은 중요하다.

notes:

Question 2 of 4

캠퍼스 외부 노래자랑 대회

전통적으로 대학 합창단은 캠퍼스에서 콘서트만 했다. 하지만, 내년부터 이 노래 동상들은 그들의 일정에 캠퍼스 외부의 경연 행사들을 추가할 것이다. 합창 단장은 노래 경연 대회에 출전하면 학생들이 자신의 능력에서 더 높은 수준을 추구하도록 동기 부여가 되기 때문에 합창단 공연의 질이 높아질 것으로 보고 있다. 또한 단장은 학교 밖에서 공연하는 합창단이 학교 음악 프로그램의 명성을 높여 프로그램이 성장하는데 도움이 되기를 바란다.

Listen to two students discussing the article.

W: Aren't you in the choir? What do you think about the announcement?

M: I actually like it!

W: Oh really?

M: Definitely. The off campus competition will definitely motivate the students.

W: How so?

M: Have you heard other schools sing? They're really good! So we would have to work hard to compete with them. Right now, we only practice once a week. But if we were to compete outside of school, we would practice more and it would help improve our singing skills.

W: That's true. After all, practice makes perfect. How about the other point the article mentions? Something about spreading the music program?

M: That's something else that's positive about this article. Right now, our music program is small. Although we have some talented singers, it would be great to recruit more talents that are out there. By attending the off campus events, people will hear how good we are and it might attract students to come to our university and become part of our choir group.

W: I guess that makes sense.

두 학생이 그 기사에 대해 토론하는 것을 들으시오.

W: 너 합창단 아냐? 그 발표에 대해 어떻게 생각해?

M: 난 사실 맘에 들어!

W: 오 그래?

M: 물론이지. 캠퍼스 외부 대회는 학생들에게 확실히 동기를 부여할 거야.

W: 어떻게?

M: 다른 학교들이 노래 부르는 거 들어 봤어? 정말 잘해! 그래서 우리가 그들과 경쟁하기 위해선 열심히 노력해야 할 거야. 지금은 일주일에 한 번만 연습해. 하지만 우리가 학교 외부에서 경쟁한다면, 우리는 더 많이 연습할 것이고 노래 실력을 향상시키는데 도움이 될 거야.

W: 맞아. 결국 연습이 완벽을 만들지. 그 기사에서 언급하는 다른 점은 어때? 음악 프로그램을 전파하는 것 같은 거 말이야.

M: 그건 이 기사의 또 다른 긍정적인 부분이야. 지금 우리의 음악 프로그램은 작아. 비록 재능 있는 가수들이 있지만, 더 많은 재능 있는 가수들을 영입하면 좋을 것 같아. 캠퍼스 외부 행사에 참여함으로써, 사람들은 우리가 얼마나 잘하는지 듣게 될 것이고, 학생들이 우리 대학에 와서 합창단의 일원이 되게 할 수 있어.

W: 그거 말 되네.

그 남자는 대학의 발표에 대해 자신의 의견을 말한다. 그의 의견과 그가 그 의견을 지지하는 근거를 설명하시오

Page.174

Question 3 of 4
잔존 행동
대부분의 경우에 동물들은 그들이 자연 서식지에서 살아남을 수 있도록 도와주는 방식으로 행동한다. 그러나, 동물은 때때로 뚜렷한 목적을 가지고 있지 않은 것 같은 행동을 보일 수도 있다. 그 행동의 원래 목적은 오래 전에 그 기능을 상실했을지도 모른다. 이러한 행동들은 잔존 행동이라고 불리며, 한때 그들의 서식지가 달랐을 때는 동물에게 유용했다. 그러나 조건의 변화로 인해, 그 행동은 의도된 목적에 부합하지 못한다. 따라서 환경 변화에 영향을 받은 행동은 잔존 행동이 되었다.

Now listen to a lecture in a biology class. A good example of an animal that shows relict behavior is found in North America, an animal called the American Pronghorn. Pronghorns are deer-like animals that live in the open grassy plains in the middle of North America. The most notable characteristic about the pronghorn is that they are really fast. Actually, they are the fastest animals in the western hemisphere. Once a pronghorn starts to run, its predators like the bobcat or coyote cannot catch up. So how did these deer like animals come to run so quickly? Well, tens of thousands of years ago, the conditions in the grassy plains were different for the pronghorns. Back then, lions used to live alongside the pronghorn in the grassy plains, chasing and hunting the pronghorns. As we all know, lions are very swift hunters, much faster than the bobcats or coyotes we find in the plains today. However, lions have become extinct in North America and no longer endanger the pronghorn. But long ago, the lions would chase the pronghorn for their meals, so the pronghorn's speed was important for its survival.	이제 생물학 수업의 강의를 들으시오. 잔존 행동을 보여주는 동물의 좋은 예는 북미에서 발견된 아메리카 영양이라는 동물입니다. 영양은 북아메리카의 한 가운데 있는 넓은 풀밭에 사는 사슴과 같은 동물이죠. 영양의 가장 눈에 띄는 특징은 정말 빠르다는 겁니다. 사실, 그들은 서반구에서 가장 빠른 동물이에요. 영양이 뛰기 시작하면, 스라소니나 코요테 같은 포식자들은 그것을 따라잡을 수 없습니다. 그렇다면 이 사슴 같은 동물이 어떻게 그렇게 빨리 달리게 되었을까요? 음, 수 만년 전만 해도, 영양들에게 초원이 많은 평원의 환경은 달랐습니다. 그 당시, 사자들은 풀이 무성한 평야에서 영양과 함께 살며, 영양을 쫓고 사냥하곤 했습니다. 우리 모두가 알다시피, 사자는 매우 빠른 사냥꾼입니다. 오늘날 우리가 평원에서 발견하는 스라소니나 코요테보다 훨씬 빠르죠. 하지만, 북아메리카에서 사자들은 멸종되었고 더 이상 영양을 위험에 빠뜨리지 않습니다. 그러나 오래 전에는 사자들이 먹잇감으로 영양을 쫓아다녔기 때문에, 영양의 속도는 그들이 생존하는데 있어 중요했습니다.

영양과 사자의 예를 들어, 잔존 행동의 개념을 설명하시오.

Question 4 of 4

Listen to a lecture from a business class.

Target customers are people who are prone to buy a company's products. The target customers actually greatly influence the company's marketing strategies. To develop their marketing strategies, a company will observe specific market customers to determine where and when to advertise so that they can market their products effectively. Today, I would like to discuss two characteristics of target customers that can influence a company's marketing strategy.

First, let's imagine a company making toy cars. Their target customers will be kids. So if a company wants to make sure that their television advertisements are viewed by kids, it would want to show their ads during the times kids watch television. That way, the company is sure that their target customers are watching their advertisements, which would result in the target customers buying their toy cars or asking their parents to buy it for them.

Second, geographic location is important in target customers, which refers to places where the customers live. For instance, if a company is selling boats, their target customers would have to live close to oceans or lakes so that they can ride the boats. I mean, there's no point in purchasing a boat if you don't live near water. So by showing advertisements along roads or on television in cities that are located next to oceans or lakes, the company will have a higher chance of reaching out to its target customers and selling more boats.

경영학 강의를 들으시오.

대상 고객은 동일한 기업의 제품들을 구매하는 경향이 있는 사람들입니다. 대상 고객들은 실제로 회사의 마케팅 전략에 큰 영향을 미치죠. 마케팅 전략을 개발하기 위해, 회사는 그들의 제품을 효과적으로 마케팅할 수 있도록 광고할 장소와 시기를 결정하기 위해 특정 시장 고객들을 관찰할 겁니다. 오늘은 기업의 마케팅 전략에 영향을 미칠 수 있는 대상 고객들의 두 가지 특성에 대해 이야기하고자 합니다.

먼저 장난감 자동차를 만드는 회사를 상상해 봅시다. 그들의 대상 고객은 아이들이 될 것입니다. 그래서 만약 어떤 회사가 그들의 텔레비전 광고를 확실히 어린이들에게 보여주고 싶다면, 아이들이 텔레비전을 보는 시간에 그들의 광고를 보여주고 싶을 겁니다. 그렇게 하면, 회사는 그들의 대상 고객들이 그들의 광고를 보고 있다는 것을 확신하게 되고, 그러면 대상 고객들이 장난감 자동차를 사거나 부모들에게 그것을 사 달라고 요구하게 될 겁니다.

둘째, 지리적 위치는 대상 고객에게 중요하며, 이는 고객이 거주하는 장소를 가리킵니다. 예를 들어, 한 회사가 보트를 판매한다면, 그들의 대상 고객들은 보트를 탈 수 있도록 바다나 호수 근처에 살아야 할 겁니다. 물가에 살지 않으면 보트를 사도 소용없다는 말이죠. 그래서 바다나 호수 옆에 위치한 도시에서 도로나 텔레비전을 통해 광고를 내보냄으로써, 이 회사는 대상 고객에게 다가가 더 많은 보트를 판매할 수 있는 더 높은 가능성을 갖게 될 겁니다.

강의의 핵심 내용과 사례를 활용하여, 대상 고객의 특성이 제품 마케팅 전략에 어떤 영향을 미치는지 설명하시오.